D0572775

A TREASURY OF POEMS FOR WORSHIP AND DEVOTION

By the same Editor

THE TABLE OF THE LORD

A TREASURY OF STORY-SERMONS FOR CHILDREN

WORSHIP RESOURCES FOR THE CHRISTIAN YEAR

THE FUNERAL ENCYCLOPEDIA

STORIES ON STONE: A BOOK OF AMERICAN EPITAPHS

TWENTIETH CENTURY BIBLE COMMENTARY (CO-EDITOR)

SPEAKER'S ILLUSTRATIONS FOR SPECIAL DAYS

TREASURY OF SERMON ILLUSTRATIONS

POEMS OF EDWIN MARKHAM

SELECTED POEMS OF JOHN OXENHAM

A TREASURY OF POEMS FOR WORSHIP AND DEVOTION

EDITED BY

Charles L. Wallis

HARPER & ROW PUBLISHERS

New York, Evanston, and London

M-Q
LIBRARY OF CONGRESS CATALOG CARD NUMBER: 59–14534

ACKNOWLEDGMENTS

Special acknowledgment is made to the following, who have granted permission for the reprinting of copyrighted material from the books and periodicals listed below:

ASSOCIATION PRESS for "O young and fearless Prophet" from *Prayers for Times Like These* by S. Ralph Harlow, copyright 1942 by Association Press

ATLANTIC MONTHLY for extract from "Invocation" by Theodore Spencer; "Prayer" by George Villiers.

BEACON PRESS for "The Prophecy Sublime" from *The Thought of God, Third Series,* by Frederick L. Hosmer, copyright by Frederick L. Hosmer.

THE BODLEY HEAD for "I dare not pray to thee, for thou art won" from *The Collected Poems of Maurice Baring;* "A Prayer" from *Orchard Songs* by Norman Gale; "A Prayer" from *New Poems* by Richard Le Gallienne; extract from "The Return" from *The Return and Other Poems* by Margaret L. Woods.

BOSTON ATHENAEUM for "The Artisan," "Hora Christi" and "Seaward Bound" from *The Road to Castaly and Later Poems* by Alice Brown.

BROADMAN PRESS for "In Time of Trouble" from *With All Thy Heart* by Leslie Savage Clark, copyright 1957 by Broadman Press.

BRUCE HUMPHRIES, INC., for "Thanksgiving" from *Altar Candles* by Susie M. Best, copyright 1927 by Richard G. Badger, reprinted by permission of Bruce Humphries, Inc.

BURNS OATES & WASHBOURNE, LTD., for "Lux in Tenebris" from *The Flower of Peace* by Katharine Tynan Hinkson; "In Time of Need" and "Passiontide Communion" from *Twilight Songs* by Katharine Tynan Hinkson; "The Folded Flock" from *Verses and Reverses* by Wilfrid Meynell.

THE CATHOLIC WORLD for "A Sailor's Prayer" by George Hornell Morris.

THE CHRISTIAN CENTURY for "Prayer" by Margueritte Harmon Bro; "Give Our Conscience Light" by Aline B. Carter; "Prayer for Light" by Stanton A. Coblentz; "Prayer" by Hazel J. Fowler; "A Litany for Old Age" and "Prayer before Meat" by Una W. Harsen; "Prayer in April" by Sara Henderson Hay; "Great Spirit of the speeding spheres" and "Thou God of all, whose presence dwells" by John Haynes Holmes; "A Prayer for Charity" by Edwin O. Kennedy; "Poet's Prayer" by Adelaide Love; "Prayer" by Barbara Marr; "Prayer" and "Prayer for the Useless Days" by Edith Love-

joy Pierce; "Prayer at Dawn" by Edwin McNeill Poteat; "A Prayer for a Preacher" by Edward Shillito; "O Christ, who died upon a cross" by John Calvin Slemp; "Prayer in a Country Church" by Ruth B. Van Dusen; "Prayer" by Amos N. Wilder.
CITY BANK OF PORTAGE, WISCONSIN, executor, for "Credo" from *The Secret Way* by Zona Gale.
THE CLARENDON PRESS for extract from "The Approach" from [Thomas] *Traherne's Poems of Felicity;* extract from "Royall Presents" from *The Poems of Nathaniel Wanley.*
THE COMMONWEAL for "A Prayer for a Marriage" by Mary Carolyn Davies; "Prayer of a Teacher" by Dorothy Littlewort.
CONSTABLE & CO., LTD., for "O martyred Spirit of this helpless Whole" from *Poems* by George Santayana, published by Charles Scribner's Sons, reprinted by permission of Constable & Co., Ltd.
THE CRESSET PRESS for "For Sleep, or Death" from *Urania* by Ruth Pitter.
J. M. DENT & SONS, LTD., for "Prayer" from *The Collected Poems of James Elroy Flecker.*
DODD, MEAD & CO., INC., for extract from "The Song of the Pilgrims" from *The Collected Poems of Rupert Brooke,* copyright © 1915 by Dodd, Mead & Co., Inc., 1943 by Edward Marsh; "Lord of the far horizons" from *Bliss Carman's Poems,* copyright © 1929 by Bliss Carman; "A Hymn" from *The Collected Poems of G. K. Chesterton,* copyright © 1932 by Dodd, Mead & Co., Inc.; extract from "De Amore" from *The Poems of Ernest Dowson,* reprinted by permission of Dodd, Mead & Co., Inc.; "Equipment" from *The Complete Poems of Paul Laurence Dunbar,* copyright by Dodd, Mead & Co., Inc.; "The Scribe's Prayer" from *Rhymes of a Rolling Stone* by Robert Service, copyright © 1912, 1940 by Robert W. Service; "The Mystic's Prayer" from *Poems* by William Sharp, reprinted by permission of Dodd, Mead & Co., Inc.
DOUBLEDAY & CO., INC., for "Father" from *The Secret and Other Poems* by Arthur Davison Ficke, copyright © 1936 by Arthur Davison Ficke, reprinted by permission of Doubleday & Co., Inc.; "Search" from *The Dark Cavalier* by Margaret Widdemer, copyright © 1958 by Margaret Widdemer, reprinted by permission of Doubleday & Co., Inc.
E. P. DUTTON & CO., INC., for "Blessing on Little Boys," "House Blessing" and "The Scribe's Prayer" from *Death and General Putnam and 101 Other Poems* by Arthur Guiterman, copyright 1935 by E. P. Dutton & Co., Inc.
GOOD HOUSEKEEPING for "I Yield Thee Praise" by Philip Jerome Cleveland.
GROVE PRESS, INC., for "Variations on a Theme by George Herbert" from *Selected Poems* by Marya Zaturenska, copyright 1954 by Marya Zaturenska Gregory.
THE FIRST PENNSYLVANIA BANKING AND TRUST CO., executor, for "Be Thou my guide, and I will walk in darkness," "A Seeker in the Night," "Suppliant" and "Thanksgiving" from *Poems* by Florence Earle Coates.
HARCOURT, BRACE AND CO., INC., for extract from "The Rock" from *The Complete Poems and Plays* by T. S. Eliot, copyright 1952, reprinted by permission of Harcourt, Brace and Co., Inc., and Faber and Faber, Ltd.; "Prayer for a New House" from *This Singing World* by Louis Untermeyer, copyright 1923 by Harcourt, Brace and Co., Inc., renewed by Louis Untermeyer, reprinted by permission of Harcourt, Brace and Co., Inc.
HARPER & BROTHERS for "Because of Thy Great Bounty" from *Light of the Years* by Grace Noll Crowell, copyright 1936 by Harper & Brothers,

reprinted by permission; "The Poet Prays" from *Silver in the Sun* by Grace Noll Crowell, copyright 1939 by Harper & Brothers, reprinted by permission; "The Litany of the Dark People" from *On These I Stand* by Countee Cullen, copyright 1947 by Harper & Brothers, reprinted by permission; extract from "The Christ of the Andes," "A Prayer" and "Shine on me, Secret Splendor" from *Poems of Edwin Markham*, copyright 1950 by Virgil Markham, reprinted by permission of Harper & Brothers; extract from "A Little Te Deum of the Commonplace," "Per Ardua ad Astra" and "The Prince of Life" from *Selected Poems of John Oxenham*, copyright 1948 by Erica Oxenham, reprinted by permission of Harper & Brothers; "Let me not die till death is due to come" from *In This Our Day* by Edith Lovejoy Pierce, copyright 1944 by Edith Lovejoy Pierce, reprinted by permission of Harper & Brothers; "O Christ, thou art within me like a sea," "Supplication" and "In the Wilderness" from *Therefore Choose Life* by Edith Lovejoy Pierce, copyright 1947 by Edith Lovejoy Pierce, reprinted by permission of Harper & Brothers; "Eternal God whose searching eye doth scan," "Grace at Evening" and "Prayer for Contentment" from *Over the Sea, the Sky* by Edwin McNeill Poteat, copyright 1945 by Harper & Brothers, reprinted by permission; "Patience" and "The Unutterable Beauty" from *The Unutterable Beauty* by G. A. Studdert-Kennedy, copyright by Harper & Brothers, reprinted by permission; "De Profundis" and "If I have lifted up mine eyes to admire" from *The Healing of the Waters* by Amos N. Wilder, copyright 1943 by Harper & Brothers, reprinted by permission; "Supplication" by Josephine Johnson and "A Prayer" by Clinton Scollard from *Harper's Magazine*.

William Heinemann, Ltd., for "The Cell" from *Escape and Fantasy* by George Rostrevor.

Henry Holt and Co., Inc., for "Idols" from *Poems of Earth's Meaning* by Richard Burton; "A Prayer in Spring" from *Complete Poems of Robert Frost*, copyright 1949 by Henry Holt and Co., Inc.; "For My Funeral" from *The Collected Poems of A. E. Housman*, copyright 1940 by Henry Holt and Co., Inc., reprinted by permission of Henry Holt and Co., Inc., Jonathan Cape, Ltd., and The Society of Authors as the literary representatives of the estate of the late A. E. Housman; "At a Window" and "Prayers of Steel" from *Complete Poems* by Carl Sandburg, copyright 1950 by Carl Sandburg, reprinted by permission of Henry Holt and Co., Inc.

Houghton Mifflin Co. for "A Communion Hymn" from *A Marriage Cycle* by Alice Freeman Palmer; "Hymn" from *The Collected Poems of Josephine Preston Peabody;* "Vespers" from *The Harvest of the Quiet Eye* by Odell Shepard; "Hymn to the West" from *The Poems of Edmund Clarence Stedman.*

The Hymn Society of America for "A Grace" by Thomas Tiplady.

Herbert Jenkins, Ltd., for extract from "A Dream of Artemis" from *The Complete Poems of Francis Ledwidge.*

Nannine Joseph, agent, for "Why, Lord, must something in us" from *Collected Poems* by Mark Van Doren, copyright 1939 by Mark Van Doren, published by Henry Holt and Co., Inc.

The Journal of the National Education Association for "Prayer of a Beginning Teacher" by Ouida Smith Dunnam.

J. B. Lippincott Co. for "Prayer for the Pilot" from *Poems* by Cecil Roberts, copyright 1920, 1947 by Cecil Roberts, reprinted by permission of J. B. Lippincott Co.

LITTLE, BROWN & CO. for "Savior! I've no one else to tell" from *Further Poems of Emily Dickinson.*

LONGMANS, GREEN & CO., INC., for "Process," "Resolution" and "Security" from *A Rime of the Rood and Other Poems* by Charles L. O'Donnell, copyright by Longmans, Green & Co., Inc.

THE MACMILLAN CO. for "I Have a Roof" from *Against the Sun* by Ada Jackson, copyright 1940 by Ada Jackson, reprinted by permission of The Macmillan Co.; "D'Alalos' Prayer" from *Poems* by John Masefield, copyright 1930 by John Masefield, reprinted by permission of The Macmillan Co., The Macmillan Co. of Canada, Ltd., The Society of Authors and John Masefield; "Grace before Sleep" and "A Prayer" from *The Collected Poems of Sara Teasdale,* copyright 1937 by The Macmillan Co.; "Prayer for Pain" from *Collected Poems of John G. Neihardt,* copyright by The Macmillan Co.; extract from "Adam's Song of the Visible World" from *Poems* by Ridgely Torrence, copyright 1941 by The Macmillan Co.; "A Chant Out of Doors" from *Bluestone* by Marguerite Wilkinson, copyright by The Macmillan Co.

MACMILLAN & CO., LTD., for "Desire" from *Selected Poems* by A. E., reprinted by permission of Diarmuid Russell, Macmillan & Co., Ltd., St. Martin's Press, Inc.; "To the Unknown Light" from *Poems, 1912–1932,* by Edward Shanks, reprinted by permission of Mrs. Shanks, Macmillan & Co., Ltd., St. Martin's Press, Inc.

MARIE RODELL AND JOAN DAVES, INC., agent, for "Prayer for Living and Dying" by Christopher La Farge from *The Saturday Review,* copyright © 1949 by Christopher La Farge.

THE NEW YORK TIMES for "Prayer for All Poets at This Time" by Irwin Edman, reprinted by permission of Mrs. Lester Markel and *The New York Times;* "Prayer in Affliction" by Violet Alleyn Storey, reprinted by permission of Violet Alleyn Storey and *The New York Times.*

W. W. NORTON & CO., INC., for "First Day of Teaching" from *Hands Laid upon the Wind* by Bonaro W. Overstreet, copyright 1955 by W. W. Norton & Co., Inc., reprinted by permission of W. W. Norton & Co., Inc.

OXFORD UNIVERSITY PRESS (London) for "Clean Hands" from *The Complete Poetical Works of Austin Dobson,* reprinted by permission of A. T. A. Dobson, executor, and Oxford University Press, publisher.

A. D. PETERS, agent, for "Almighty God, whose justice like a sun" from *Sonnets and Verse* by Hilaire Belloc, published by Sheed and Ward, Inc., reprinted by permission of A. D. Peters.

RAND MCNALLY & CO. (CONKEY DIVISION) for extract from "The Christian's New-Year Prayer" and "Uselessness" from *Collected Poems of Ella Wheeler Wilcox.*

RANDOM HOUSE, INC., for extract from "For the Time Being" from *The Collected Poems of W. H. Auden,* copyright 1945 by W. H. Auden, reprinted by permission of Random House, Inc., and Faber and Faber, Ltd.

THE REILLY & LEE CO., INC., for "Grace at Evening" from *Collected Verse of Edgar A. Guest,* copyright 1934 by The Reilly & Lee Co.

RINEHART & CO., INC., for extract from "Impiety" from *Change of Season* by Helene Magaret, copyright 1941 by Helene Magaret, reprinted by permission of Rinehart & Co., Inc.; "At Cockcrow" from *A Wayside Lute* by Lizette Woodworth Reese, copyright 1909, 1937 by Lizette Woodworth Reese, reprinted by permission of Rinehart & Co., Inc.; "Prayer of an Unbeliever" from *Pastures and Other Poems* by Lizette Woodworth Reese, copyright 1933 by Lizette Woodworth Reese, reprinted by permission of Rinehart & Co., Inc.

THE RYERSON PRESS for "The Fallen" from *Selected Poems of Duncan Campbell Scott,* copyright 1951 by The Ryerson Press.

SAMUEL FRENCH, LTD., for "Prayer" by Eduard Mörike, tr. by John Drinkwater, from *New Poems* by John Drinkwater, reprinted by permission of Samuel French, Ltd.

THE SATURDAY REVIEW for "Prayer for the Age" by Myron H. Broomell; "Prayer by Moonlight" by Roberta Teale Swartz.

CHARLES SCRIBNER'S SONS for "A Birthday Prayer" from *John Finley: Poems,* copyright 1941 by Charles Scribner's Sons, reprinted by permission of Charles Scribner's Sons; "Valley of the Shadow" from *Verses New and Old* by John Galsworthy, copyright 1926 by Charles Scribner's Sons, 1940 by Ada Galsworthy, reprinted by permission of Charles Scribner's Sons, William Heinemann, Ltd.; extract from "Thanks from Earth to Heaven" from *Dust and Light* by John Hall Wheelock, copyright 1919 by Charles Scribner's Sons, 1947 by John Hall Wheelock, reprinted by permission of Charles Scribner's Sons.

SIDGWICK & JACKSON, LTD., for "Petition" and "A Prayer" from *Poems, 1908–1919,* by John Drinkwater; "Dedication," "The Gardener" and "Spikenard" from *The Collected Poems of Laurence Housman.*

THE SOCIETY OF AUTHORS for "Dust to Dust" and "The Scribe" from *Collected Poems, 1901–1918,* by Walter de la Mare, published by Henry Holt and Co., Inc., reprinted by permission of the literary trustees of Walter de la Mare, The Society of Authors as their representative, and Violet F. Barton.

ALAN SWALLOW CO. for "A Prayer for My Son" from *Collected Poems* by Yvor Winters, copyright 1952 by Yvor Winters, reprinted by permission of Alan Swallow, publisher.

THE VIKING PRESS, INC., for "Envoy" from *St. Peter Relates an Incident* by James Weldon Johnson, copyright 1917, 1921, 1935 by James Weldon Johnson, reprinted by permission of The Viking Press, Inc.; "A Prayer" from *Swords for Life* by Irene Rutherford McLeod, copyright 1916 by B. W. Huebsch, reprinted by permission of The Viking Press, Inc., Chatto and Windus, Ltd.; "The Need" from *Sequences* by Siegfried Sassoon, reprinted by permission of The Viking Press, Inc.; "A Prayer for 1936" from *Rhymed Ruminations* by Siegfried Sassoon, reprinted by permission of The Viking Press, Inc.

YALE UNIVERSITY PRESS for "The World's Desire" from *The Falconer of God* by William Rose Benét; "Prayer against Indifference" from *Letter to a Comrade* by Joy Davidman.

BEATRIX ALDENHAM for "Homo Factus Est," "Requests" and "Strange, all-absorbing Love, who gatherest" from *The Poems of Digby Mackworth Dolben.*

CHARLES ANGOFF for his poem, "Litany," from *The American Mercury.*

JOSEPH AUSLANDER for his poem, "A Prayer for Thanksgiving," from *The New York Times.*

KARLE WILSON BAKER for her poem, "Let me grow lovely, growing old," from *Dreamers on Horseback.*

FRANCIS H. BANGS for "Thanksgiving Day" from *The Foothills of Parnassus* by John Kendrick Bangs.

Christy MacKaye Barnes for extract from "A Prayer of the Peoples" from *Poems and Plays* by Percy MacKaye.
Edmund Blunden for his poem, "A Psalm," from *The Poems of Edmund Blunden.*
Walter Russell Bowie for his poem, "God of the Nations, who from dawn of days," from *Social Hymns.*
George S. Burgess for "For Deeper Life" and "Thou knowest, Thou who art the soul of all" from *Selected Poems of Katharine Lee Bates.*
Hazel David Clark for "Common Blessings" and "Wanderers" from *God's Dreams* by Thomas Curtis Clark.
W. W. Coblentz for "The Housewife" by Catherine Cate Coblentz.
Caroline W. Driscoll for "Grace for Gardens" from *Garden Grace* by Louise Driscoll.
Stephen P. Dunn for his poem, "Prayer of the Young Stoic," from *The Saturday Review.*
Max Eastman for "A Hymn to God in Time of Stress" from *Poems of Five Decades,* copyright 1954 by Max Eastman, published by Harper & Brothers.
Edwin Essex for his poem, "Loneliness."
Hildegarde Flanner for her poem, "Prayer for This Day," from *Poetry.*
Harry Emerson Fosdick for his poems, "O God, in restless living" and "The Prince of Peace his banner spreads," from *Praise and Service.*
Margery Freeman for "A Soldier's Prayer" from *The Land I Live In* by Robert Freeman.
Winfred Ernest Garrison for his poem, "Thy sea, O God, so great," from *The Christian Century*
Grace Guiney for "An Outdoor Litany" and "Deo Optimo Maximo" from *Happy Ending* by Louise Imogen Guiney.
Hermann Hagedorn for his poem, "Prayer during Battle," from *Ladders through the Blue.*
Mary L. Ham for "A Prayer" from *Songs of the Spirit* by Marion Franklin Ham.
Leslie Pinckney Hill for his poem, "The Teacher."
Elizabeth J. Huckel for "O mind of God, broad as the sky" by Oliver Huckel.
Barbara Benson Jefferys for "O Thou whose gracious presence blest" by Louis F. Benson, from *Christian Song.*
Edith Jewett for "In the Dark" from *The Poems of Sophie Jewett.*
Victoria Saffelle Johnson for her poem, "Dedication," from *The Golden Book of Catholic Poetry.*
Blanche Mary Kelly for her poems, "The Mirror," from *America;* "Omniscience," from *The Valley of Vision.*
Harry Kemp for his poems, "A Seaman's Confession of Faith," from *Chanteys and Ballads;* "To God, the Architect," from *The Poet's Life of Christ.*
Elinor Lennen for her poem, "Prayer for a Play House," from *The New York Sun.*
Francis A. Litz for "Insomnia," "Missing" and "To the Christ" from *The Poetry of Father Tabb.*
John L. MacDonnell for "Plea for Hope" by Francis Carlin.
Seamus MacManus for "Mea Culpa" from *The Four Winds of Eirinn* by Ethna Carbery.
Ellen C. Masters for "Schofield Hurley" from *Spoon River Anthology*

by Edgar Lee Masters; "Supplication" from *Blood of the Prophets* by Edgar Lee Masters.

KATHLEEN MAYNARD for "Faith's Difficulty" from *Poems* by Theodore Maynard.

ERNEST MERRILL for "Not alone for mighty empire" by William Pierson Merrill from *Social Hymns.*

ELIZABETH K. MORTON for "Touring" from *Ships in Harbour* by David Morton.

ELLA H. MYER for "The Poet" and "Thanksgiving" from *Utterance and Other Poems* by Angela Morgan.

JOHNSTONE G. PATRICK for his poems, "Closing Prayer," "Grace" and "Prayer for Peace," from *Above the Thorn.*

LEROY PRATT PERCY for extract from "Epilogue," "Hymn to the Sun" and "A Page's Road Song" from *The Collected Poems of William Alexander Percy.*

MARY L. ROBBINS for "Put forth, O God, Thy Spirit's might," "Saviour, whose love is like the sun" and "Spirit from whom our lives proceed" from *The Way of Light* by Howard Chandler Robbins.

THEODORE ROETHKE for his poem, "Prayer before Study," from *Open House.*

E. MERRILL ROOT for his poem, "Prayer for Dreadful Morning," from *Bow of Burning Gold.*

MARGARET E. SANGSTER for her poem, "A Mother's Prayer."

ALMA JOHNSON SARETT for "Let Me Flower as I Will," "Let me go down to dust and dreams" and "Wind in the Pine" from *The Collected Poems of Lew Sarett,* copyright 1941 by Henry Holt and Co., Inc., copyright transferred 1944 to Alma Johnson Sarett.

EDITH G. SCHLOERB for "O Thou Eternal Source of Life" and "Thou Light of Ages, Source of living truth" by Rolland W. Schloerb.

RALPH W. SEAGER for his poem, "The Taste of Prayer," from *Beyond the Green Gate.*

ORA SEARLE for "An Easter Canticle" and "A Prayer for the Old Courage" from *Selected Poems of Charles Hanson Towne.*

ELEANOR SLATER for her poems, "Petition," from *Quest;* "Sight and Insight," from *Why Hold the Hound?*

FLORENCE SPRING-RICE for extract from "In Memoriam, A.C.M.L." from *Poems* by Cecil Arthur Spring-Rice.

MARIE PEARY STAFFORD for "Invocation" from *The Land We Love* by Wendell Phillips Stafford.

WILLIAM FORCE STEAD for his poem, "How Infinite Are Thy Ways," from *Uriel.*

CHARLES WHARTON STORK for his poem, "God, You have been too good to me," from *The New York Sun.*

A. M. SULLIVAN for his poem, "Psalm to the Holy Spirit," from *Psalms of the Prodigal.*

MARY DIXON THAYER for her poem, "A Prayer."

VIOLET ALLEYN STOREY for her poems, "A Prayer after Illness," "A Prayer for the New Year" and "A Prayer in Late Autumn," from *Green of the Year.*

GILBERT THOMAS for his poems, "The Cup of Happiness" and "Invocation," from *Selected Poems.*

JEAN STARR UNTERMEYER for her poems, "Last Plea," "The Passionate Sword" and "Sung on a Sunny Morning," from *Love and Need.*

Acknowledgments

HAROLD VINAL for his poem, "Hymnal," from *The Compass Eye*.
CLAIRE WHITAKER for "Out-of-Doors" and "Worship" from *The Call of the Human* by Robert Whitaker.
GLORIA G. WOOD for "A Prayer in Time of Blindness" by Clement Wood from *Survey Magazine*.

For my wife
Betty Watson Wallis

CONTENTS

PREFACE

Readers of our generation are stubbornly convinced that they prefer prose to poetry. For this reason the discovery of the salutary adventures which verse affords is more exciting than in a poetry-saturated period. But true religion has always found poetry to be a vehicle through which its teachings and aspirations are best expressed. The artistic, rhythmical, and imaginative element in poetry heightens spiritual insight, deepens emotional responsiveness, and broadens a sympathetic communication of the common affirmations of faith.

This volume depicts man's "keen, enormous, haunting, never-sated thirst for God" in the poetic form and manner of prayer as developed in the Hebrew-Christian devotional heritage. It also reflects attitudes toward the Eternal which vary from bold rebellion to quiet fellowship. The editor anticipates that here may be found vessels from which readers shall drink deeply to discover renewed inspiration in familiar lines and challenge and help in less-known words. The abiding joy of poetry is the reader's identification with a writer's mind and the realization that the poet has skillfully interpreted his needs and aspirations.

The prayer-poems in this volume have been selected on the bases of clarity of thought, communicability, and general excellence of content and expression. Although esoteric and obscure verses have been omitted, a number of the poems will require an alert thoughtfulness and a co-operative partnership with the poets if the most satisfying rewards and stimulating values are to be gained. Vigorous and elevating poems have been preferred to sentimental and shallow verses, and all of the poems included are worth reading, not only once, but again and again.

To bring together many splendid and forgotten poems, while not arbitrarily rejecting the better-known poems a reader would expect to find in a volume such as this, has been a controlling purpose in the making of this collection. More than 60 per cent of these poems are not listed in *Granger's Index to Poetry,* a nearly complete tabulation of anthologized verse.

All poems, except the one numbered 298, have been transcribed without alteration or adaptation from original, standard, or authorized publications. No attempt has been made to modernize the wording and spelling of the original texts of the older poets, although the standard and available publications of a few of the seventeenth-century poets indicate their editors' hand. First lines have been used when poets have not assigned titles.

The editor is appreciative of the generous assistance offered by the personnel of many libraries, in particular, the University of Rochester Library, the Rochester Public Library, the Colgate Rochester Divinity School Library, the New York Public Library, the New York State Library, the Library of Congress, the Union Theological Seminary Library, the Princeton Theological Seminary Library, and most especially the Cornell University Library. Many rare books have been made available through Interlibrary Loan, and the editor is greatly indebted to the cordial co-operation of Mrs. Frances V. Wilkins, Keuka College librarian, and her associates.

C. L. W.

Keuka College
Keuka Park, New York

I

THE POET'S PETITION

1 *The Unutterable Beauty*

God, give me speech, in mercy touch my lips,
I cannot bear Thy Beauty and be still,
Watching the red-gold majesty that tips
The crest of yonder hill,
And out to sea smites on the sails of ships,

That flame like drifting stars across the deep,
Calling their silver comrades from the sky,
As long and ever longer shadows creep,
To sing their lullaby,
And hush the tired eyes of earth to sleep.

Thy radiancy of glory strikes me dumb,
Yet cries within my soul for power to raise
Such miracles of music as would sum
Thy splendour in a phrase,
Storing it safe for all the years to come.

O God, Who givest songs too sweet to sing,
Have mercy on Thy servant's feeble tongue,
In sacrificial silence sorrowing,
And grant that songs unsung,
Accepted at Thy mercy-seat, may bring

New light into the darkness of sad eyes,
New tenderness to stay the stream of tears,
New rainbows from the sunshine of surprise,
To guide men down the years,
Until they cross the last long bridge of sighs.

G. A. Studdert-Kennedy

2 *A Dedication*

Life of my learning, fire of all my Art,
O thou to whom my days obscurely tend,
Dear past expression, friend beyond a friend,
Soul of my soul and heart within my heart,

Hear and forgive thy servant over bold
Who dared to write the words he could not say,
And with too eager hand hath given away
That which his eyes alone to thee unfold!

Mary Elizabeth Coleridge

3 *The Scribe's Prayer*

Help me to hold the Vision Undefiled,
To love, and, taught by Love, to understand;
Lord, as a father with a backward child,
Guide Thou the pen within my wavering hand!

Arthur Guiterman

4 *Envoy*

If homely virtues draw from me a tune
In jingling rhyme—or in ambitious rune;
Or if the smoldering future should inspire
My hand to try the seer's prophetic lyre;
Or if injustice, brutishness, and wrong
Stir me to make a weapon of my song;

O God, give beauty, truth, strength to my words—
Oh, may they fall like sweetly cadenced chords,
Or burn like beacon fires from out the dark,
Or speed like arrows, swift and sure to the mark.

James Weldon Johnson

5 *A Prayer*

Father in Heaven! from whom the simplest flower
On the high Alps or fiery desert thrown,
Draws not sweet odour or young life alone,
But the deep virtue of an inborn power
To cheer the wanderer in his fainting hour,
With thoughts of Thee; to strengthen, to infuse
Faith, love, and courage, by the tender hues
That speak Thy presence; oh! with such a dower
Grace Thou my song!—the precious gift bestow
From Thy pure Spirit's treasury divine,
To wake one tear of purifying flow,
To soften one wrung heart for Thee and thine;
So shall the life breathed through the lowly strain,
Be as the meek wild-flower's—if transient, yet not vain.

Felicia Dorothea Hemans

6 *Poet's Prayer*

Not from my reverent sires hath come
  My faith, O Living God, in Thee;
Not from Thy prophet's ageless words
  Spoken however verily;

But from the intimate things that pass
  Between us, Father, through the days.
Thyself hath shown my God to me
  A thousand times, a thousand ways.

Thy love hath been conspicuous
  In every hour, a steadfast sign;
From this the certainty, from this
  The deep assurance that is mine.

Yet more I ask—Oh give me words,
  Lord God, again and yet again

To sing my faith! To sing my faith
Unto the hearts of men!

Adelaide Love

7 *Hymn*

Dear Lord, Whose serving-maiden
I hope one day to be,
Touch Thou mine ears that they may hear,
Mine eyes that they may see;
And let my words and thoughts shine white
With Thy divinity.

Dear Lord, Whose child I am, Whose Heir
I hope one day to be,
Give light to all belovèd ones;
Give Bread to them, and me.
And keep all evil from us here,
And some beyond the sea.

Dear Lord, Whose faithful Singer
I hope one day to be,
Wing all my songs, as Thou canst do,
With Love and melody;
And bid them fly unto the day
That Thou hast need of me.

Josephine Preston Peabody

8 *A Prayer*

To Thy continual Presence, in me wrought,
Vainly might I, a fallen creature, say
Through Thee, Thou essence of Creation's thought,
That I partake the blessedness of Day;
That on my verse might fall Thy healing dew!
And all its faults obscure, its charms renew.

I praise Thee—not because Thou needest praise
(What were my thanks? Thou needest not my lays)—
Yet will I praise Thee—for Thou art the fire
That sparkles on the strings of my dark lyre.

Sole Majesty! around us softly flowing,
Unseen, yet in the common sunset glowing!
Fate of the Universe! the Tide of things!
Sacred alike to all beneath Thy wings.

If Passion's trance lay on my writing clear,
Then should I see Thee, evident and near;
Passion—that breath of Instinct, and the key
Of Thy dominions, untold Majesty!

William Ellery Channing

9 *To Musicke Bent*

To Musicke bent is my retyred minde,
And faine would I some song of pleasure sing;
But in vaine ioys no comfort now I finde,
From heau'nly thoughts all true delight doth spring.
Thy power, O God, thy mercies, to record,
Will sweeten eu'ry note and eu'ry word.

All earthly pompe or beauty to expresse,
Is but to carue in snow, on waues to write.
Celestiall things, though men conceiue them lesse,
Yet fullest are they in themselues of light:
Such beames they yeeld as know no meanes to dye,
Such heate they caste as lifts the Spirit high.

Thomas Campion

10 *The Poet Prays*

The crushing of a thousand petals, Lord,
Distills one drop of essence from a flower.

Crush me, Oh God, if thereby my song makes
Some tired heart walk with beauty for an hour.

If under bruising pestles I give voice
To the high white rapture of a faint perfume,
And catching it, one weary of paved ways
Turns back to a lost path where wood violets bloom.

If I can bring the quick relief of tears
To dry eyes dulled with bitterness for long,
Gather the fragrant petals of my life
And crush them, Lord, then help me sing the song.

Grace Noll Crowell

11 From *The Poet*

Why hast thou breathed, O God, upon my thoughts
And tuned my pulse to thy high melodies,
Lighting my soul with love, my heart with flame,
Thrilling my ear with songs I cannot keep—
Only to set me in the market-place
Amid the clamor of the bartering throng,
Whose ears are deaf to my impassioned plea,
Whose hearts are heedless of the word I bring?

And yet—dear God, forgive! I will sing on.
I will sing on until that shining day
When one perchance—one only it may be—
Shall turn aside from out the sordid way,
List'ning with eager ears that understand.

Angela Morgan

12 *Prayer for Song*

Mend my broken mood,
Maker of Life and Song,

Lest this interlude
Of silence be too long.

Call my soul awake,
Set my heart aflame!
Singing fire will make
Ash of sloth and shame.

Touch my lips with song,
Wing my words with good.
Shepherd of things gone wrong,
Mend my broken mood.

Fay Lewis Noble

13 *Spikenard*

As one who came with ointments sweet,
  Abettors to her fleshly guilt,
And brake and poured them at Thy Feet,
  And worshipped Thee with spikenard spilt:
So from a body full of blame,
And tongue too deeply versed in shame,
Do I pour speech upon Thy Name.
O Thou, if tongue may yet beseech,
Near to Thine awful Feet let reach
This broken spikenard of my speech!

Laurence Housman

14 *His Prayer for Absolution*

For Those my unbaptized Rhimes,
Writ in my wild unhallowed Times;
For every sentence, clause and word,
That's not inlaid with Thee, (my Lord)
Forgive me God, and blot each Line
Out of my Book, that is not Thine.

But if, 'mongst all, thou find'st here one
Worthy thy Benediction;
That One of all the rest, shall be
The Glory of my Work, and Me.

Robert Herrick

15 *Grace*

Before Reading Emily Brontë's Poems

Good God of scholar, simpleton, and sage!
Bless Thou the stoic tears upon each page—
The poet's heart bowed and bared,
The temple rent,
The bread broken and shared,
The young life spent.
Each storm-wracked phrase, each fiery-furnaced word,
Bless to our use, as we peruse, O Lord!

Johnstone G. Patrick

16 *The Scribe's Prayer*

When from my fumbling hand the tired pen falls,
And in the twilight weary droops my head;
While to my quiet heart a still voice calls,
Calls me to join my kindred of the Dead:
Grant that I may, O Lord, ere rest be mine,
Write to Thy praise one radiant, ringing line.

For all of worth that in this clay abides,
The leaping rapture and the ardent flame,
The hope, the high resolve, the faith that guides:
All, all is Thine, and liveth in Thy name:
Lord, have I dallied with the sacred fire?
Lord, have I trailed Thy glory in the mire!

E'en as a toper from the dram-shop reeling,
Sees in his garret's blackness, dazzling fair,
All that he might have been, and, heart-sick, kneeling,

Sobs in the passion of a vast despair:
So my ideal self haunts me alway—
When the accounting comes, how shall I pay?

For in the dark I grope, nor understand;
And in my heart fight selfishness and sin:
Yet, Lord, I do not seek Thy helping hand;
Rather let me my own salvation win:
Let me through strife and penitential pain
Onward and upward to the heights attain.

Yea, let me live my life, its meaning seek;
Bear myself fitly in the ringing fight;
Strive to be strong that I may aid the weak;
Dare to be true—O God! the Light, the Light!
Cometh the Dark so soon. I've mocked Thy Word,
Yet do I know Thy Love: have mercy, Lord . . .

Robert Service

17 *The Scribe*

What lovely things
Thy hand hath made:
The smooth-plumed bird
In its emerald shade,
The seed of the grass,
The speck of stone
Which the wayfaring ant
Stirs—and hastes on!

Though I should sit
By some tarn in thy hills,
Using its ink
As the spirit wills
To write of Earth's wonders,
Its live, willed things,

Flit would the ages
  On soundless wings
Ere unto Z
  My pen drew nigh;
Leviathan told,
  And the honey-fly:
And still would remain
  My wit to try—
My worn reeds broken,
  The dark tarn dry,
All words forgotten—
  Thou, Lord, and I.
Walter de la Mare

18 From *Eternall Mover*

Eternall mover, whose diffused glory,
  To shew our grovelling reason what thou art,
Unfolds itself in clouds of nature's story,
  Where man, thy proudest creature, acts his part,
Whom yet, alas! I know not why, we call
The world's contracted sum, the little all;

For what are we but lumps of walking clay?
  Why should we swel? whence should our spirits rise?
Are not bruit beasts as strong, and birds as gay,
  Trees longer liv'd, and creeping things as wise?
Only our souls was left an inward light,
To feel our weaknes, and confess thy might.

Thou, then, our strength, father of life and death,
  To whom our thanks, our vows, ourselves we ow,
From me, thy tenant of this fading breath,
  Accept those lines which from thy goodnes flow;
And thou, that wert thy regal prophet's Muse,
Do not thy praise in weaker strains refuse.

Let these poor notes ascend unto thy throne,
  Where majesty doth sit, with mercy crown'd,
Where my redeemer lives, in whom alone
  The errours of my wandring life are drown'd,
Where all the quire of heav'n resound the same,
That only thine, thine is the saving name.

Henry Wotton

19 *Prayer for All Poets at This Time*

Angel of poets,
Tell us how
To reach men simply,
To reach them now,
Never forgetting
The curve of song
In the jagged passion
For righting wrong.

Knowing we need
(However pure
Our song, our singing)
A theme that's sure,
Its burden brave
And its substance true,
Forever ancient,
Forever new,
Speaking straight to the mind
Of horror faced,
Of blessings blurred,
And of dreams debased.

Singing firmly, too,
Of hope undeterred,
Of the dreaming risk
By faith incurred,

Of heavens bought
At a daring price,
Paid well in advance
With sacrifice.

Angel of poets,
Tell us how
To move men nobly,
To move them now.

Irwin Edman

20 *Prayer*

As I walk through the streets
I think of the things
That are given to my friends:
Myths of old Greece and Egypt,
Greek flowers, Greek thoughts,
And all that incandescence,
All that grace,
Which I refuse.

If even the orchards of England,
Its garden and its woods,
Its fields and its hills,
Its rivers and its seas,
Were mine;
But they are not.

But these are nothing.
Give me the flame, O Gods,
To light these people with,
These pavements, this motor traffic,
These houses, this medley.

Give me the vision,
And they may live.

Frank Stewart Flint

II

TO GOD THE FATHER

1 · PORTALS OF PRAISE

21 *Hymn*

Lord, with glowing heart I'd praise thee
  For the bliss thy love bestows,
For the pardoning grace that saves me,
  And the peace that from it flows.
Help, O God! my weak endeavor,
  This dull soul to rapture raise;
Thou must light the flame, or never
  Can my love be warmed to praise.

❉

Lord! this bosom's ardent feeling
  Vainly would my lips express;
Low before thy foot-stool kneeling,
  Deign thy suppliant's prayer to bless.
Let thy grace, my soul's chief treasure,
  Love's pure flame within me raise;
And, since words can never measure,
  Let my life show forth thy praise.

Francis Scott Key

22 From *The Rock*

  O Light Invisible, we praise Thee!
Too bright for mortal vision.
O Greater Light, we praise Thee for the less;
The eastern light our spires touch at morning,
The light that slants upon our western doors at evening,
The twilight over stagnant pools at batflight,
Moon light and star light, owl and moth light,
Glow-worm glowlight on a grassblade.
O Light Invisible, we worship Thee!

We thank Thee for the lights that we have kindled,
The light of altar and of sanctuary;
Small lights of those who meditate at midnight
And lights directed through the coloured panes of windows
And light reflected from the polished stone,
The gilded carven wood, the coloured fresco.
Our gaze is submarine, our eyes look upward
And see the light that fractures through unquiet water.
We see the light but see not whence it comes.
O Light Invisible, we glorify Thee!

T. S. Eliot

23

Light of the World

Light of the world, we hail Thee
  Flushing the eastern skies:
Never shall darkness veil Thee
  Again from human eyes;
Too long, alas, withholden,
  Now spread from shore to shore;
Thy light, so glad and golden,
  Shall set on earth no more.

Light of the world, Thy beauty
  Steals into every heart,
And glorifies with duty
  Life's poorest, humblest part;
Thou robest in Thy splendor
  The simplest ways of men,
And helpest them to render
  Light back to Thee again.

Light of the world, before Thee
  Our spirits prostrate fall;
We worship, we adore Thee,
  Thou light, the life of all;
With Thee is no forgetting
  Of all Thine hand hath made;

Thy rising hath no setting,
 Thy sunshine hath no shade.

Light of the world, illumine
 This darkened land of Thine,
Till everything that's human
 Be filled with the divine;
Till every tongue and nation,
 From sin's dominion free,
Rise in the new creation
 Which springs from love and Thee.

John S. B. Monsell

24 *O Thou Whose Pow'r*

O thou whose pow'r o'er moving worlds presides,
Whose voice created, and whose wisdom guides,
On darkling man in pure effulgence shine,
And clear the clouded mind with light divine.
'Tis thine alone to calm the pious breast
With silent confidence and holy rest:
From thee, great God, we spring, to thee we tend,
Path, motive, guide, original, and end.

Boethius
Tr. Samuel Johnson

25 *A Sun-day Hymn*

Lord of all being! throned afar,
Thy glory flames from sun and star;
Centre and soul of every sphere,
Yet to each loving heart how near!

Sun of our life, thy quickening ray
Sheds on our path the glow of day;
Star of our hope, thy softened light
Cheers the long watches of the night.

Our midnight is thy smile withdrawn;
Our noontide is thy gracious dawn;
Our rainbow arch thy mercy's sign;
All, save the clouds of sin, are thine!

Lord of all life, below, above,
Whose light is truth, whose warmth is love,
Before thy ever-blazing throne
We ask no lustre of our own.

Grant us thy truth to make us free,
And kindling hearts that burn for thee,
Till all thy living altars claim
One holy light, one heavenly flame!

Oliver Wendell Holmes

26 *Psalm LXXXIV*

How lovely are thy dwellings fair!
  O Lord of hosts, how dear
The pleasant tabernacles are!
  Where thou dost dwell so near.
My soul doth long and almost die
  Thy courts O Lord to see,
My heart and flesh aloud do cry,
  O living God, for thee.
There even the sparrow freed from wrong
  Hath found a house of rest,
The swallow there, to lay her young
  Hath built her brooding nest,
Even by thy altars Lord of hosts
  They find their safe abode,
And home they fly from round the coasts
  Toward thee, my king, my God.
Happy, who in thy house reside
  Where thee they ever praise,

Happy, whose strength in thee doth bide,
  And in their hearts thy ways.
They pass through Baca's thirsty vale,
  That dry and barren ground
As through a fruitful watery dale
  Where springs and showers abound.
They journey on from strength to strength
  With joy and gladsome cheer
Till all before our God at length
  In Sion do appear.
Lord God of hosts hear now my prayer
  O Jacob's God give ear,
Thou God our shield look on the face
  Of thy anointed dear.
For one day in thy courts to be
  Is better, and more blest
Than in the joys of vanity,
  A thousand days at best.
I in the temple of my God
  Had rather keep a door,
Than dwell in tents, and rich abode
  With sin forevermore.
For God the Lord both sun and shield
  Gives grace and glory bright,
No good from them shall be withheld
  Whose ways are just and right.
Lord God of hosts that reignest on high,
  That man is truly blest,
Who only on thee doth rely,
  And in thee only rest.

John Milton

27 From *Our Heavenly Father*

My God! how wonderful Thou art,
  Thy Majesty how bright,

How beautiful Thy Mercy-Seat
In depths of burning light!

How dread are Thine eternal years,
O everlasting Lord!
By prostrate spirits day and night
Incessantly adored!

How beautiful, how beautiful
The sight of Thee must be,
Thine endless wisdom, boundless power,
And awful purity!

Oh how I fear Thee, living God!
With deepest, tenderest fears,
And worship Thee with trembling hope,
And penitential tears.

Yet I may love Thee too, O Lord!
Almighty as Thou art,
For Thou hast stooped to ask of me
The love of my poor heart.

Frederick William Faber

28 *I Yield Thee Praise*

For thoughts that curve like winging birds
Out of the summer dusk each time
I drink the splendor of the sky
And touch the wood-winds swinging by—
I yield Thee praise.

For waves that lift from autumn seas
To spill strange music on the land,
The broken nocturne of a lark
Flung out upon the lonely dark—
I yield Thee praise.

For rain that piles gray torrents down
Black mountain-gullies to the plain,
For singing fields and crimson flare
At daybreak, and the sea-sweet air—
I yield Thee praise.

For gentle mists that wander in
To hide the tired world outside
That in our hearts old lips may smile
Their blessing through life's afterwhile—
I yield Thee praise.

For hopes that fight like stubborn grass
Up through the clinging snows of fear
To find the rich earth richer still
With kindliness and honest will—
I yield Thee praise.

Philip Jerome Cleveland

29 *"Who Wert and Art and Evermore Shalt Be"*

Bring, O Morn, thy music! Bring, O night, thy hushes!
Oceans, laugh the rapture to the storm-winds coursing free!
Suns and stars are singing, Thou art our Creator,
Who wert and art and evermore shalt be!

Life and Death, thy creatures, praise thee, Mighty Giver!
Praise and prayer are rising in thy beast and bird and tree:
Lo! they praise and vanish, vanish at thy bidding,—
Who wert and art and evermore shalt be!

Light us! lead us! love us! cry thy groping nations,
Pleading in the thousand tongues but naming only thee,
Weaving blindly out thy holy, happy purpose,—
Who wert and art and evermore shalt be!

Life nor Death can part us, O thou Love Eternal,
Shepherd of the wandering star and souls that wayward flee!
Homeward draws the spirit to thy Spirit yearning,—
Who wert and art and evermore shalt be!

William Channing Gannett

30 From *Psalm VIII*

Lord what is man, that he should find
A place in his Creator's mind
Or what his whole increase—
A race of rebels vain and weak,
That he should for a moment break
Upon his Saviour's peace?

An angel quite thou mad'st him not,
A little lower is his lot,
On earth thou set'st him down;
There his dominion and degree,
To glorify and worship thee
For glory and a crown.

Him thou deputed to review
The scenes of nature, and subdue
Thy creatures to his will;
Whose motley numbers own his sway,
And by his strength compell'd obey,
Or disciplin'd by skill.

All flocks of sheep and droves of kine,
Which as his olive and his vine,
To man their goodness yield;
And not a beast that can be nam'd,
But may be taken or be tam'd
In woodland or in field.

In air, in ocean he controuls,
The feather'd millions, finny shoals,
From minnows to the whale;
Whate'er beneath the waters creep,
Or glide within the yielding deep,
Or on the surface sail.

O thou that rul'st the human heart,
Supreme of nature and of art,
How is thy name renown'd!
How blest thy providential care,
In heav'n above, in earth and air,
And in the vast profound!

Christopher Smart

31

Lord of My Heart's Elation

Lord of my heart's elation,
Spirit of things unseen,
Be thou my aspiration
Consuming and serene!

Bear up, bear out, bear onward
This mortal soul alone,
To selfhood or oblivion,
Incredibly thine own,—

As the foamheads are loosened
And blown along the sea,
Or sink and merge forever
In that which bids them be.

I, too, must climb in wonder,
Uplift at thy command,—
Be one with my frail fellows
Beneath wind's strong hand,

A fleet and shadowy column
Of dust or mountain rain,
To walk the earth a moment
And be dissolved again.

Be thou my exaltation
Or fortitude of mien,
Lord of the world's elation
Thou breath of things unseen!

Bliss Carman

32 *Adam's Song of the Visible World*

Praise, O my heart, with praise from depth and height
To you, O Source of Life. How very great
The glories are that beat upon my sight
From you, so robed with honor and the weight
Of majesty, who clothe yourself with light
As with a garment, veiling you from us.

❉

Your glory is forever and with dance
You move among your works and they to you.
You look upon the earth and at your glance
It sways with trembling and above the hills
A smoke ascends where you have touched their rest.
I will sing praises to you while life fills
My flesh with breath; as long as life shall stream
From you within me, I will sing your light.
May all my thoughts and all I dare in dream
Be true to you, acceptable and blest.
You are my tide of joy, my sea, my shore,
My field of sky with stars that never set,
And I will learn your wonders all my days,
Let me remember you in pain and let
The spirit of denial vanish quite
From earth and be forgotten in its ways,
And my blind ways in darkness be no more.

Ridgely Torrence

33 From *Passage to India*

Bathe me O God in thee, mounting to thee,
I and my soul to range in range of thee.

O Thou transcendent,
Nameless, the fibre and the breath,
Light of the light, shedding forth universes, thou centre of them,
Thou mightier centre of the true, the good, the loving,
Thou moral, spiritual fountain—affection's source—thou
 reservoir,
(O pensive soul of me—O thirst unsatisfied—waitest not there?
Waitest not haply for us somewhere there the Comrade perfect?)
Thou pulse—thou motive of the stars, suns, systems,
That, circling, move in order, safe, harmonious,
Athwart the shapeless vastnesses of space,
How should I think, how breathe a single breath, how speak, if
 out of myself,
I could not launch, to those, superior universes?

Walt Whitman

34 *So Far, So Near*

Thou, so far, we grope to grasp thee—
Thou, so near, we cannot clasp thee—
Thou, so wise, our prayers grow heedless—
So, so loving, they are needless!
In each human soul thou shinest.
Human-best is thy divinest.
In each deed of love thou warmest;
Evil into good transformest.
Soul of all, and moving centre
Of each moment's life we enter.
Breath of breathing—light of gladness—
Infinite antidote of sadness;—
All-preserving ether flowing

Through the worlds, yet past our knowing.
Never past our trust and loving,
Nor from thine our life removing.
Still creating, still inspiring,
Never of thy creatures tiring.
Artist of thy solar spaces,
And thy humble human faces;
Mighty glooms and splendors voicing;
In thy plastic work rejoicing;
Through benignant law connecting
Best with best—and all perfecting,
Though all human races claim thee,
Thought and language fail to name thee,
Mortal lips be dumb before thee,
Silence only may adore thee!

Christopher Pearse Cranch

35 *Hymn*

Father, we come not as of old,
  Distrustful of Thy Law,
Hoping to find Thy seamless robe
  Marred by some sudden flaw,—
Some rent to let Thy glory through
  And make our darkness shine,
If haply thus our souls may know
  What power and grace are Thine.

Thy seamless robe conceals Thee not
  From earnest hearts and true;
The glory of Thy perfectness
  Shines all its texture through;
And on its trailing hem we read,
  As Thou dost linger near,
The message of a love more deep
  Than any depth of fear.

And so no more our hearts shall plead
  For miracle and sign;
Thy order and Thy faithfulness
  Are all in all divine:
These are Thy revelations vast
  From earliest days of yore;
These are our confidence and peace;
  We cannot wish for more.

John W. Chadwick

36

Inspiration

Life of Ages, richly poured,
Love of God, unspent and free,
Flowing in the Prophet's word
And the People's liberty!

Never was to chosen race
That unstinted tide confined;
Thine is every time and place,
Fountain sweet of heart and mind!

Secret of the morning stars,
Motion of the oldest hours,
Pledge through elemental wars
Of the coming spirit's powers!

Rolling planet, flaming sun,
Stand in nobler man complete;
Prescient laws Thine errands run,
Frame the shrine for Godhead meet.

Homeward led, the wandering eye
Upward yearned in joy or awe,
Found the love that waited nigh,
Guidance of Thy guardian Law.

In the touch of earth it thrilled;
Down from the mystic skies it burned;
Right obeyed and passion stilled
It eternal gladness earned.

Breathing in the thinker's creed,
Pulsing in the hero's blood,
Nerving simplest thought and deed,
Freshening time with truth and good,

Consecrating art and song,
Holy book and pilgrim track,
Hurling floods and tyrant wrong
From the sacred limits back,—

Life of Ages, richly poured,
Love of God, unspent and free,
Flow still in the Prophet's word,
And the People's liberty!

Samuel Johnson

37 *Through Unknown Paths*

O thou who art of all that is
  Beginning both and end,
We follow thee through unknown paths,
  Since all to thee must tend:
Thy judgments are a mighty deep
  Beyond all fathom-line;
Our wisdom is the childlike heart,
  Our strength, to trust in thine.

We bless thee for the skies above,
  And for the earth beneath,
For hopes that blossom here below
  And wither not with death;

But most we bless thee for thyself,
O heavenly Light within,
Whose dayspring in our hearts dispels
The darkness of our sin.

Be thou in joy our deeper joy,
Our comfort when distressed;
Be thou by day our strength for toil,
And thou by night our rest.
And when these earthly dwellings fail
And Time's last hour is come,
Be thou, O God, our dwelling-place
And our eternal home!

Frederick L. Hosmer

2 · MAN'S INSATIABLE QUEST

38 *The World's Desire*

Pain of too poignant beauty fills the heart
  Seeing rich dreams through some rare sunset drift,
  Or when on lawns the summer shadows shift
In soft designs beyond Man's clumsy art
To emulate. Quick tears may almost start
  When the anointed stars to heaven uplift
  Their voice adoration, and a rift
Seems shining in the night where pale clouds part.

In hours like these what vast benevolence
  Breathes through the world! O God beyond illusion,
  Then we divine thou knowest our dark confusion,
With fervent answers soothing every sense;
And yet we feel—what pain—in the intense
  Desire for thee to end thy long seclusion!

William Rose Benét

39 *Lord, If Thou Art Not Present*

Lord, if Thou art not present, where shall I
  Seek Thee the absent? If Thou art not everywhere,
How is it that I do not see Thee nigh?

Thou dwellest in a light remote and fair.
  How can I reach that light, Lord? I beseech
Thee, teach my seeking, and Thyself declare

Thyself the sought to me. Unless Thou teach
  Me, Lord, I cannot seek; nor can I find
Thee, if Thou wilt not come within my reach.

Lord, let me seek, with sturdy heart and mind,
  In passion of desire and longingly.
Let me desire Thee, seeking Thee; and find—
  Loving Thee, find Thee; love Thee, finding Thee.

John Gray

40 From *Emblem VII, Book III*

Wherefore hidest thou thy face, and holdest me for thine enemy? Job 13:24

Why dost Thou shade Thy lovely face? Oh why
Does that eclipsing hand so long deny
The sunshine of Thy soul-enlivening eye?

Without that light, what light remains in me?
Thou art my life, my way, my light; in Thee
I live, I move, and by Thy beams I see.

Thou art my life: if Thou but turn away,
My life's a thousand deaths; Thou art my way:
Without Thee, Lord, I travel not, but stray.

My light Thou art: without Thy glorious sight,
My eyes are darkened with perpetual night.
My God, Thou art my way, my life, my light.

Thou art my way: I wander if Thou fly;
Thou art my light: if hid, how blind am I!
Thou art my life: if Thou withdraw, I die.

Mine eyes are blind and dark, I cannot see;
To whom, or whither, should my darkness flee,
But to the light? and who's that light but Thee?

My path is lost, my wandering steps do stray;
I cannot safely go, nor safely stay;
Whom should I seek but Thee, my path, my way?

Francis Quarles

41

Search

Where shall we find Thee—where art Thou, O God?
For Thou hast taken away our signs from us,
Discredited the guides we thought from Thee,
And we have only left to show the way
A voice—the wavering voice that cries in us
Once in a long, long while, when soul and sense
Clasp for a moment and Thy light shines through:
We can be only sure of one thing now,
Our little fevered hearts that endlessly
Toss up and down upon the waves of the world—
Where shall we find Thee? Where art Thou, O God?

Where shall we find Thee? Where art Thou, O God?
Thou who perhaps may yet be, not now made,
Thou who perhaps hast been and art not now,
Thou whose last echoings across our hearts
Perhaps may not be known nor wondered of
By our young children—Thou, our God of old,
God of Forever—Speak to us again!
Give us some little loving sign again
That we may see Thee through the glass of it,
Come in some kindly human shape we know.
Our eyes are dazzled now with staring long
Through bleak, bright lights unknown, unhumanized,
Thy love seems not for us, it shines so far,
Not such as we can dare exchange with Thee.

Where can we find Thee? Where art Thou, O God?
Though I should take away your little lights from you,
My little silver spinning coin the moon,
My little burning beat of time the sun,
And all my life and yours have passed beyond
To whirling chains of planets not yet more
Than flying vapors now—still I shall be
And ye shall be with Me.

Margaret Widdemer

42

From *Uriel*

I thought the night without a sound was falling,
But standing still,
No stem or leaf I stirred;
Under the hedge a cricket chirred,
A robin woke the silence calling,
An owl went hovering by,
Hunting the spacious twilight with tremulous cry.
Far off where woods were dark,
A ranging dog began to bark,
A heifer lowed upon the lone-tree hill.

I had not known were I not still
How infinite are Thy ways.
I wondered what Thy life could be,
O Thou aloof Immensity;
Voice after voice, and every voice was Thine.
So I stood wondering,
Until a child began to sing,
Going late home, awed by the gathering haze.
I said, Her life at one with mine,
Is also Thine;
But compassing Thy many voices now,
Here, for a moment, I am Thou.

William Force Stead

43

From *Hymn from the French of Lamartine*

O Thou who bidst the torrent flow,
  Who lendest wings unto the wind,—
Mover of all things! where art Thou?
  Oh, whither shall I go to find
The secret of Thy resting-place?
  Is there no holy wing for me,
That, soaring, I may search the space
  Of highest heaven for Thee?

Oh, would I were as free to rise
As leaves on autumn's whirlwind borne,—
The arrowy light of sunset skies,
Or sound, or ray, or star of morn,
Which melts in heaven at twilight's close,
Or aught which soars unchecked and free
Through earth and heaven; that I might lose
Myself in finding Thee!

John Greenleaf Whittier

44 *The Quest*

I cannot find Thee! Still on restless pinion
My spirit beats the void where Thou dost dwell;
I wander lost through all Thy vast dominion,
And shrink beneath Thy light ineffable.

I cannot find Thee! E'en when most adoring
Before Thy throne I bend in lowliest prayer;
Beyond these bounds of thought, my thought upsoaring
From farthest quest comes back; Thou art not there.

Yet high above the limits of my seeing,
And folded far within the inmost heart,
And deep below the deeps of conscious being,
Thy splendor shineth; there, O God, Thou art.

I cannot lose Thee! Still in Thee abiding
The end is clear, how wide soe'er I roam;
The Hand that holds the worlds my steps is guiding,
And I must rest at last, in Thee, my home.

Eliza Scudder

45 *If There Had Anywhere Appeared*

If there had anywhere appeared in space
Another place of refuge, where to flee,

Our hearts had taken refuge in that place,
And not with Thee.

For we against creation's bars had beat
Like prisoned eagles, through great worlds had sought
Though but a foot of ground to plant our feet,
Where Thou wert not.

And only when we found in earth and air,
In heaven or hell, that such might nowhere be—
That we could not flee from Thee anywhere,
We fled to Thee.

Richard Chenevix Trench

46 From *The Song of the Pilgrims*

O Thou
God of all long desirous roaming,
Our hearts are sick of fruitless homing,
And crying after long desire.
Hearten us onward! as with fire
Consuming dreams of other bliss.
The best Thou givest, giving this
Sufficient thing—to travel still
Over the plain, beyond the hill,
Unhesitating through the shade,
Amid the silence unafraid,
Till, at some sudden turn, one sees
Against the black and muttering trees
Thine altar, wonderfully white,
Among the Forests of the Night.

Rupert Brooke

47 *Desire*

With Thee a moment! Then what dreams have play!
Traditions of eternal toil arise,

Search for the high, austere and lonely way
The Spirit moves in through eternities.
Ah, in the soul what memories arise!

And with what yearning inexpressible,
Rising from long forgetfulness I turn
To Thee, invisible, unrumoured, still:
White for Thy whiteness all desires burn.
Ah, with what longing once again I turn!

George William Russell (A. E.)

48 *To-Morrow*

Lord, what am I, that, with unceasing care,
Thou didst seek after me, that thou didst wait,
Wet with unhealthy dews, before my gate,
And pass the gloomy nights of winter there?
Oh, strange delusion, that I did not greet
Thy blest approach! and oh, to Heaven how lost,
If my ingratitude's unkindly frost
Has chilled the bleeding wounds upon thy feet!
How oft my guardian angel gently cried,
"Soul, from thy casement look, and thou shalt see
How he persists to knock and wait for thee!"
And, oh! how often to that voice of sorrow,
"'To-morrow we will open," I replied,
And when the morrow came I answered still, "To-morrow."

Lope de Vega
Tr. by Henry Wadsworth Longfellow

49 *To My God*

Oh how oft I wake and find
I have been forgetting thee!
I am never from thy mind:
Thou it is that wakest me.

George Macdonald

50 *Prayer*

Bear with me, Master, when I turn from Thee.
Pity me in my loss.
Forgive me, knowing I shall come again
As certainly as day that follows night.
Steel magnetized will ever seek the pole,
So I, of my free will which is not free,
But in its very nature bent to Thine,
Will come to rest in Thee.
I, the swinging needle in the compass of the world;
Thou, the perpetual North.

Edith Lovejoy Pierce

51 *Sight and Insight*

I could not see You with my eyes.
  I stared, but could not see.
I could not pierce the dim disguise
  Of any Mystery.

At last I did not try to see.
  Instead, I knelt apart
And loved the Dark. Then suddenly
  I saw You with my heart.

Eleanor Slater

52 *To Heaven*

Good, and great God, can I not thinke of thee,
But it must, straight, my melancholy bee?
Is it interpreted in me disease,
That, laden with my sinnes, I seeke for ease?
O, be thou witnesse, that the reynes dost know,
And hearts of all, if I be sad for show,
And judge me after: if I dare pretend
To ought but grace, or ayme at other end.

As thou art all, so be thou all to mee,
First, midst, and last, converted one, and three;
My faith, my hope, my love: and in this state,
My judge, my witnesse, and my advocate.
Where have I beene this while exil'd from thee?
And whither rap'd, now thou but stoup'st to mee?
Dwell, dwell here still: O, being every-where,
How can I doubt to finde thee ever, here?
I know my state, both full of shame, and scorne,
Conceiv'd in sinne, and unto labour borne,
Standing with feare, and must with horror fall,
And destin'd unto judgement, after all.
I feele my griefes too, and there scarce is ground,
Upon my flesh t'inflict another wound.
Yet dare I not complaine, or wish for death
With holy Paul, lest it be thought the breath
Of discontent; or that these prayers bee
For wearinesse of life, not love of thee.

Ben Jonson

53 From *For Communion with God*

Alas, my God, that we should be
  Such Strangers to each other!
O that as Friends we might agree,
  And walk, and talk together!
Thou know'st my Soul does dearly love
  The Place of thine Abode;
No Music drops so sweet a Sound
  As these two Words, *My God.*

⁜

When wilt thou come unto me, Lord,
  For 'till thou dost appear,
I count each Moment for a Day,
  Each Minute for a Year:

Come, Lord, and never from me go,
This World's a darksome Place;
I find no pleasure here below,
When thou dost veil thy Face.

Thomas Shepherd

54 From *New Hymns for Solitude*

I found Thee in my heart, O Lord,
As in some secret shrine;
I knelt, I waited for Thy word,
I joyed to name Thee mine.

I feared to give myself away
To that or this; beside
Thy altar on my face I lay,
And in strong need I cried.

Those hours are past. Thou art not mine,
And therefore I rejoice,
I wait within no holy shrine,
I faint not for the voice.

In Thee we live; and every wind
Of heaven is Thine; blown free
To west, to east, the God unshrined,
Is still discovering me.

Edward Dowden

55 *Credo*

O you not only worshipful but dear
Now have I learned not merely majesty
But gentleness and friendlihood to be
Your way of drawing near.

And late, upon a blue and yellow day,
Wandering alone along a hill of Spring

I caught another tender summoning,
As if you were the comrad of my play.

How strange that I have looked so lone and far
When it is you, Great Love, who lonely are.
How I have sought you in your cosmic leisure
When you are eager in my childish pleasure.

Why there is no dim doctrine to believe!
Only to feel this touching at my sleeve.

Zona Gale

56 *After St. Augustine*

Sunshine let it be or frost,
  Storm or calm, as Thou shalt choose;
Though Thine every gift were lost,
  Thee thyself we could not lose.

Mary Elizabeth Coleridge

3 · WHEN TAUGHT BY NEED

57 *A Prayer*

My God (oh, let me call Thee mine,
  Weak, wretched sinner though I be),
My trembling soul would fain be Thine;
  My feeble faith still clings to Thee.

Not only for the past I grieve,
  The future fills me with dismay;
Unless Thou hasten to relieve,
  Thy suppliant is a castaway.

I cannot say my faith is strong,
  I dare not hope my love is great;
But strength and love to Thee belong:
  Oh, do not leave me desolate!

I know I owe my all to Thee;
  Oh, *take* the heart I cannot give;
Do Thou my Strength, my Saviour be,
  And *make* me to Thy glory live!

Anne Brontë

58 *Lord of the Winds*

Lord of the winds, I cry to Thee,
    I that am dust,
  And blown about by every gust
    I fly to Thee.

Lord of the waters, unto Thee I call.
  I that am weed upon the waters borne,

And by the waters torn,
Tossed by the waters, at Thy feet I fall.
Mary Elizabeth Coleridge

59 *Supplication*

Here where no increase is,
Blossom, nor bud, nor fruit—
Scattered the pregnant seed,
Withered the sturdy root—
Lord, for my desperate need,
Help me to compass this:

Out of the twisted heart,
Out of the bleeding side,
Out of each empty hand
Fashion me something for pride—
Something enduring, to stand
Living, vital, apart!

Something that is not I,
But born of my dearth and pain—
By the suns I never knew
Made strong for the lashing rain.
Holding both honey and dew
Up to a tenderer sky—

Holding them not in vain!
Josephine Johnson

60 *An Outdoor Litany*

The spur is red upon the briar,
The sea-kelp whips the wave ashore;
The wind shakes out the coloured fire
From lamps a-row on the sycamore;

The bluebird with his flitting note
Shows to wild heaven his wedding-coat;
The mink is busy; herds again
Go hillward in the honeyed rain;
The midges meet. I cry to Thee
Whose heart
Remembers each of these: Thou art
My God who hast forgotten me!

Bright from the mast, a scarf unwound,
The lined gulls in the offing ride;
Along an edge of marshy ground
The shad-bush enters like a bride.
Yon little clouds are washed of care
That climb the blue New England air,
And almost merrily withal
The hyla tunes at evenfall
His oboe in a mossy tree.
So too,
Am I not Thine? Arise, undo
This fear Thou hast forgotten me.

Happy the vernal rout that come
To their due offices to-day,
And strange, if in Thy mercy's sum,
Excluded man alone decay.
I ask no triumph, ask no joy,
Save leave to live, in law's employ.
As to a weed, to me but give
Thy sap! lest aye inoperative
Here in the Pit my strength shall be:
And still
Help me endure the Pit, until
Thou wilt not have forgotten me.

Louise Imogen Guiney

61 *Lord, Save Us, We Perish*

O Lord, seek us, O Lord, find us
In Thy patient care;
Be Thy Love before, behind us,
Round us, everywhere:
Lest the god of this world blind us,
Lest he speak us fair,
Lest he forge a chain to bind us,
Lest he bait a snare.
Turn not from us, call to mind us,
Find, embrace us, bear;
Be Thy Love before, behind us,
Round us, everywhere.

Christina G. Rossetti

62 *Litany*

When the sun rises on another day
Of broken hopes, vain yearnings, and futile waiting,
And hearts get a little colder
And love more distant than the most distant star
And even sleep begins to lose its small solace—
O Lord, remember me.

When the vast unreason of the immemorial sequence,
Strife and peace and more strife,
Engulfs us with such calm and mocking disregard,
And all dreams and aspirations
Lose their ultimate comfort—
O Lord, remember us.

When the smiles of children, the final support,
Recede and join the independent throng,
Leaving us with the one certainty
That they too will soon

Wait for answers that never come—
O Lord, remember us.

When death comes with false friendliness,
Bringing an end to nothing
And no future intimations
Save the repetition of this life
But on the scale of a worm—
O Lord, remember us.

Charles Angoff

63

Suppliant

Father, I lift my hands to Thee:
Reject me not!
Mine eyes are blind, I cannot see.
Be Thou the lamp unto my feet,—
Guide to the rock of my retreat;
O Light, my darkness cries to Thee!
Reject me not!

Father, mine eyes with tears are wet,
Reject me not!
Though Thou forgive, shall I forget?
Nay, though thy mercy fall like rain,
My spirit still must bear the pain
And burden of a vast regret.
Reject me not!

To whom, unfriended, should I flee?
Reject me not!
To whom, my Father, but to Thee?—
Ah! 't was thy child forgave the sin
Of the repentant Magdalen,
And blessed the thief on Calvary!—
Reject me not!

Florence Earle Coates

64 *My Soul Doth Pant Towards Thee*

My soul doth pant towards thee,
My God, source of eternal life:
Flesh fights with me;
O end the strife
And part us, that in peace I may
Unclay
My wearied spirit, and take
My flight to thy eternal spring;
Where, for his sake
Who is my King,
I may wash all my tears away
That day.
Thou conqueror of death,
Glorious triumpher o'er the grave,
Whose holy breath
Was spent to save
Lost mankind; make me to be styl'd
Thy child:
And take me, when I die,
And go unto my dust, my soul,
Above the sky
With saints enrol,
That in thy arms, for ever, I
May lie.

Jeremy Taylor

65 *The Desponding Soul's Wish*

My spirit longeth for thee,
Within my troubled breast;
Altho' I be unworthy
Of so divine a guest.

Of so divine a guest,
Unworthy tho' I be;

Yet has my heart no rest,
  Unless it come from thee.

Unless it come from thee,
  In vain I look around;
In all that I can see,
  No rest is to be found.

No rest is to be found,
  But in thy blessed love;
O! let my wish be crown'd,
  And send it from above!

John Byrom

66 *None Other Lamb, None Other Name*

None other Lamb, none other Name,
  None other Hope in heaven or earth or sea,
None other Hiding-place from guilt and shame,
    None beside Thee.

My faith burns low, my hope burns low,
  Only my heart's desire cries out in me
By the deep thunder of its want and woe,
    Cries out to Thee.

Lord, Thou art Life tho' I be dead,
  Love's Fire Thou art, however cold I be:
Nor heaven have I, nor place to lay my head,
    Nor home, but Thee.

Christina G. Rossetti

67 *To God*

Lord, I am like to Misletoe,
Which has no root, and cannot grow,
Or prosper, but by that same tree
It clings about; so I by Thee.

What need I then to feare at all,
So long as I about Thee craule?
But if that Tree sho'd fall, and die,
Tumble shall heav'n, and down will I.

Robert Herrick

68 *Spirit from Whom Our Lives Proceed*

Spirit from whom our lives proceed,
In whom is strength, through whom is power,
Be with us in this blessed hour
With gifts according to our need.

Wisdom we need, to tread aright
The paths our feet have still to learn;
And understanding to discern
The way that leadeth into light.

Counsel we need and ghostly strength
To conquer Satan and his wiles,
And though a smiling world beguiles,
Steadfast to tread our journey's length.

Knowledge and godliness are Thine:
O hear our prayer, and make them ours!
That neither pride in all its powers,
Nor sloth, may quench the light divine.

But most, O mighty Breath of God!
We pray Thee for the holy fear
That in dread reverence holds Thee dear,
And marks the path Thy saints have trod.

O Breath of God! be Thine the praise;
Be Thou the glory and the grace,
Until in our Redeemer's face
We read the meaning of our days.

Howard Chandler Robbins

4 · THE HAND THAT GUIDES

69 From *An Invocation*

O God, unknown, invisible, secure,
Whose being by dim resemblances we guess,
Who in man's fear and love abidest sure,
Whose power we feel in darkness and confess!

Without Thee nothing is, and Thou art nought
When on Thy substance we gaze curiously:
By Thee impalpable, named Force and Thought,
The solid world still ceases not to be.

Lead Thou me God, Law, Reason, Duty, Life!
All names for Thee alike are vain and hollow—
Lead me, for I will follow without strife;
Or, if I strive, still must I blindly follow.

John Addington Symonds

70 *The Pillar of the Cloud*

Lead, Kindly Light, amid the encircling gloom,
    Lead Thou me on!
The night is dark, and I am far from home—
    Lead Thou me on!
Keep Thou my feet; I do not ask to see
The distant scene,—one step enough for me.

I was not ever thus, nor pray'd that Thou
    Shouldst lead me on.
I loved to choose and see my path; but now
    Lead Thou me on!
I loved the garish day, and, spite of fears,
Pride ruled my will: remember not past years.

So long Thy power hath blest me, sure it still
    Will lead me on,
O'er moor and fen, o'er crag and torrent, till
    The night is gone;
And with the morn those angel faces smile
Which I have loved long since, and lost awhile.

John Henry Newman

71

A Hymn

After reading "Lead, Kindly Light"

Lead gently, Lord, and slow,
    For oh, my steps are weak,
And ever as I go,
    Some soothing sentence speak;

That I may turn my face
    Through doubt's obscurity
Toward thine abiding-place,
    E'en tho' I cannot see.

For lo, the way is dark;
    Through mist and cloud I grope,
Save for that fitful spark,
    The little flame of hope.

Lead gently, Lord, and slow,
    For fear that I may fall;
I know not where to go
    Unless I hear thy call.

My fainting soul doth yearn
    For thy green hills afar;
So let thy mercy burn—
    My greater, guiding star!

Paul Laurence Dunbar

72 From *Emblem III, Book IV*

Great All in All, that art my rest, my home;
My way is tedious, and my steps are slow:
Reach forth Thy helpful hand, or bid me come;
I am Thy child, O teach Thy child to go;[1]
Conjoin Thy sweet commands to my desire,
And I will venture, though I fall or tire.

Francis Quarles

73 *To His Ever-Loving God*

Can I not come to Thee, my God, for these
So very-many-meeting hindrances,
That slack my pace; but yet not make me stay?
Who slowly goes, rids (in the end) his way.
Cleere Thou my paths, or shorten Thou my miles,
Remove the barrs, or lift me o're the stiles:
Since rough the way is, help me when I call,
And take me up; or els prevent the fall.
I kenn my home; and it affords some ease,
To see far off the smoaking Villages.
Fain would I rest; yet covet not to die,
For feare of future-biting penurie:
No, no, (my God) Thou know'st my wishes be
To leave this life, not loving it, but Thee.

Robert Herrick

74 *At Cockcrow*

The stars are gone out spark by spark;
A cock crows; up the cloudy lane,
A cart toils creaking through the dark:
Lord, in Thy sight all roads are plain,
Or run they up or down,

[1] Walk

Sheep-tracks, highways to town,
Or even that little one,
Beneath the hedge, where seldom falls the sun.

If it were light, I would go west;
I would go east across the land;
But it is dark; I needs must rest
Till morn breaks forth on every hand:
Lord, choose for me,
The road that runs to Thee.

Lizette Woodworth Reese

75

In the Wilderness

Our steps are scattered far,
Confusion blurs our sight;
Lord, make our way secure
Within the ultimate light.

Strange is the lurid sky,
Unrecognized the ground;
O Lord, be lost with us,
And then we shall be found.

Edith Lovejoy Pierce

76

Seaward Bound

Give me, in this inconstant ebb and flow,
Some fixèd spot
Where I may plant the soul's desire, and know
It withers not.

An argosy, swift under purple sail,
Down sweeps the dawn,
Unloading all her spices to the gale,
And is withdrawn;
Yet no more sudden than the jewelled tower
And front of day

Falls noiseless, gem from gem, at twilight's hour
And floats away.

Even that solemn star, the beacon blaze
On reefs of night,
Wanes to a close when most the shipwrecked gaze
Implores her light.

Love hath his funeral rites at Fancy's tomb;
And friendship's gate
Swings from within, to exiles making room
For newer state.

O Thou, the Author of this whirling world,
Create for me
Some sea of being where still sails are furled
Eternally.

Or in that houseless mote, my drifting heart,
Raise Thou a throne:
Spread silence round Thee, and dwell there apart,
Awful, alone.

Alice Brown

77 From *De Amore*

Lord over life and all the ways of breath,
Mighty and strong to save
From the devouring grave;
Yea, whose dominion doth out-tyrant death,
Thou who art life and death in one,
The night, the sun;
Who art, when all things seem:
Foiled, frustrate and forlorn, rejected of to-day
Go with me all my way,
And let me not blaspheme.

Ernest Dowson

78

A Prayer

Often the western wind has sung to me,
There have been voices in the streams and meres,
And pitiful trees have told me, God, of Thee:
And I heard not. Oh! open Thou mine ears.

The reeds have whispered low as I passed by,
"Be strong, O friend, be strong, put off vain fears,
Vex not thy soul for doubts, God cannot lie":
And I heard not. Oh! open Thou mine ears.

There have been many stars to guide my feet,
Often the delicate moon, hearing my sighs,
Has rent the clouds and shown a silver street;
And I saw not. Oh! open Thou mine eyes.

Angels have beckoned me unceasingly,
And walked with me; and from the sombre skies
Dear Christ Himself has stretched out hands to me;
And I saw not. Oh! open Thou mine eyes.

Alfred Bruce Douglas

79

Psalm to the Holy Spirit

Be near to me, O white shadowless Light of my soul's swift venture.
Or, being near, be known to me who wanders in lonesome marshes
Tempted beyond my depth by a lure, the will-o'-the-wisp of error,
Taunted beyond my reach for the stars by the sorcerer's blinking
symbols.
Intimate stranger amid Love's neglect, pursue me into the grotto
Where the mind is a hive of gathering doubts, and my pulse the
hammer of anguish.
Companion of frugal hours of praise, I shall spurn the crust of the
cynic
To feast at the table of light amid mourners and misers of wisdom.

Be near to me and be known to me, primordial Eye of the Heavens,
Shaper of souls ere the hand of the Father shaped the wet clay of Adam,
First meaning of meanings when desire burst from the pods of infinite silence,
Behold me, the querulous child, pulling the edges of light for an answer,
"What shall a creature pay Thee in love for the moment of understanding?"

A. M. Sullivan

80 *Per Pacem ad Lucem*

I do not ask, Oh Lord, that life may be
A pleasant road;
I do not ask that Thou wouldst take from me
Aught of its load;

I do not ask that flowers should always spring
Beneath my feet;
I know too well the poison and the sting
Of things too sweet.

For one thing only, Lord, dear Lord, I plead,
Lead me aright—
Though strength should falter, and though heart should bleed—
Through Peace to Light.

I do not ask, Oh Lord, that Thou shouldst shed
Full radiance here;
Give but a ray of peace, that I may tread
Without a fear.

I do not ask my cross to understand,
My way to see—
Better in darkness just to feel Thy hand
And follow Thee.

Joy is like restless day; but peace divine
Like quiet night:
Lead me, Oh Lord—till perfect Day shall shine,
Through Peace to Light.

Adelaide Anne Procter

81 *The Great River*

"In la sua volontade è nostra pace."

O mighty river! strong, eternal Will,
Wherein the streams of human good and ill
Are onward swept, conflicting, to the sea,
The world is safe because it floats in Thee.

Henry van Dyke

82 *Keep Thou My Way, O Lord*

Keep thou my way, O Lord;
Myself I cannot guide;
Nor dare I trust my erring steps
One moment from Thy side;
I cannot think aright,
Unless inspired by Thee;
My heart would faint without Thy aid;
Choose Thou my thoughts for me.

For every act of faith,
And every pure design,—
For all of good my soul can know,
The glory, Lord, be Thine;
Free grace my pardon seals,
Thro' Thy atoning blood;
Free grace the full assurance brings
Of peace with Thee, my God.

O speak, and I will hear;
Command, and I obey;

My willing feet with joy will haste
  To run the heavenly way;
Keep Thou my wandering heart,
  And bid it cease to roam;
O bear me safe o'er death's cold wave
  To heaven, my blissful home.

Fanny Crosby

83 ## *Thy Way, Not Mine*

Thy way, not mine, O Lord,
  However dark it be!
Lead me by Thine own hand,
  Choose out the path for me.

Smooth let it be or rough,
  It will be still the best;
Winding or straight, it leads
  Right onward to Thy rest.

I dare not choose my lot;
  I would not, if I might:
Choose Thou for me, my God,
  So shall I walk aright.

The kingdom that I seek
  Is Thine; so let the way
That leads to it be Thine,
  Else I must surely stray.

Take Thou my cup, and it
  With joy or sorrow fill,
As best to Thee may seem;
  Choose Thou my good or ill.

Choose Thou for me my friends,
  My sickness or my health;

Choose Thou my cares for me,
  My poverty or wealth.

Not mine, not mine the choice,
  In things or great or small;
Be Thou my guide, my strength,
  My wisdom and my all.

Horatius Bonar

84 *Per Ardua ad Astra*

Life me, O God, above myself,—
Above my highest spheres,
Above the thralling things of sense
To clearer atmospheres.

Lift me above the little things,—
My poor sufficiencies,
My perverse will, my lack of zeal,
My inefficiencies;—

Above the earth-born need that gropes,
With foolish hankerings,
About earth's cumbered lower slopes
For earthly garnerings.

Above the vanities and cates
Of the Forbidden Land;—
Above the passions and the hates
That flame there hand in hand.

Lift me, O God, above myself,
Above these lesser things,
Above my little gods of clay,
And all their capturings.

And grant my soul a glad new birth,
And fledge it strong new wings,

That it may soar above the earth
To nobler prosperings.

Lift me, O God, above myself,
That, in Thy time and day,
I somewhat grace Thy fosterings
And climb Thy loftier Way.

John Oxenham

5 · HIS LOVING-KINDNESS

85 From *The Divine Wooer*

Me Lord? can'st Thou mispend
One word, misplace one look on me?
Call'st Thy love, Thy friend?
Can this poor soul the object be
Of these love-glasses, those life-kindling eyes?
What! I the centre of Thy arms embraces?
Of all Thy labour I the prize?
Love never mocks, Truth never lies.
Oh how I quake: Hope fear, fear hope displaces:
I would but cannot hope: such wondrous love amazes.

Phineas Fletcher

86 *Pro Libra Mea*

O Lord whose mercy never fails,
Weigh me on thine eternal scales,
And I am naught:
Yet load me so with grace
Of deed and thought
That I may look the balance in the face,
To note each day my gain or loss,
And lift my heart or bear my cross.

Joseph I. C. Clarke

87 *Father, How Wide Thy Glories Shine*

Father, how wide thy glories shine,
God of the universe, and mine!
Thy goodness watches o'er the whole,
As all mankind were but one soul,

Yet keeps my every sacred hair,
As I remain'd thy single care.

Charles Wesley

88 From *The Shadow and the Light*

All souls that struggle and aspire,
All hearts of prayer by thee are lit;
And, dim or clear, thy tongues of fire
On dusky tribes and twilight centuries sit.

Nor bounds, nor clime, nor creed thou know'st,
Wide as our need thy favors fall;
The white wings of the Holy Ghost
Stoop, seen or unseen, o'er the heads of all.

John Greenleaf Whittier

89 *The Pursuit*

Lord! what a busy, restless thing
Hast Thou made man!
Each day and hour he is on wing,
Rests not a span;
Then having lost the sun and light,
By clouds surpris'd,
He keeps a commerce in the night
With air disguis'd.
Hadst Thou given to this active dust
A state untir'd,
The lost son had not left the husk,
Nor home desir'd.
That was Thy secret, and it is
Thy mercy too;
For when all fails to bring to bliss,
Then this must do.
Ah, Lord! and what a purchase will that be,
To take us sick, that sound would not take Thee.

Henry Vaughan

90 *O God! Have Mercy, in This Dreadful Hour*

O God! have mercy, in this dreadful hour,
On the poor mariner; In comfort here,
Safe sheltered as I am, I almost fear
The blast that rages with resistless power.
What were it now to toss upon the waves,
The maddened waves, and know no succor near;
The howling of the storm alone to hear,
And the wild sea that to the tempest raves;
To gaze amid the horrors of the night,
And only see the billow's gleaming light;
Then, in the dread of death, to think of her,
Who, as she listens sleepless to the gale,
Puts up a silent prayer, and waxes pale?
O God! have mercy on the mariner!

Robert Southey

91 *Thy Sea So Great*

Thy sea, O God, so great,
My boat so small.
It cannot be that any happy fate
Will me befall
Save as Thy goodness opens paths for me
Through the consuming vastness of the sea.

Thy winds, O God, so strong,
So slight my sail.
How could I curb and bit them on the long
And salty trail,
Unless Thy love were mightier than the wrath
Of all the tempests that beset my path?

Thy world, O God, so fierce,
And I so frail.

Yet, though its arrows threaten oft to pierce
    My fragile mail,
Cities of refuge rise where dangers cease,
Sweet silences abound, and all is peace.

Winfred Ernest Garrison

92

A Prayer

O Lord, the hard-won miles
  Have worn my stumbling feet:
Oh, soothe me with thy smiles,
  And make my life complete.

The thorns were thick and keen
  Where'er I trembling trod;
The way was long between
  My wounded feet and God.

Where healing waters flow
  Do thou my footsteps lead.
My heart is aching so;
  Thy gracious balm I need.

Paul Laurence Dunbar

93

Love and Discipline

Since in a land not barren still,
—Because Thou dost Thy grace distil—
My lot is fall'n, bless'd be Thy will!

And since these biting frosts but kill
Some tares in me which choke, or spill
That seed Thou sow'st, bless'd be Thy skill!

Bless'd be Thy dew, and bless'd Thy frost,
And happy I to be so cross'd,
And cur'd by crosses at Thy cost.

The dew doth cheer what is distress'd,
The frosts ill weeds nip, and molest;
In both Thou work'st unto the best.

Thus while Thy sev'ral mercies plot,
And work on me now cold, now hot,
The work goes on, and slacketh not;

For as Thy hand the weather steers,
So thrive I best, 'twixt joys and tears,
And all the year have some green ears.

Henry Vaughan

94 From *Andrew Rykman's Prayer*

Pardon, Lord, the lips that dare
Shape in words a mortal's prayer!

❉

Not as one who seeks his home
With a step assured I come;
Still behind the tread I hear
Of my life-companion, Fear;
Still a shadow deep and vast
From my westering feet is cast,
Wavering, doubtful, undefined,
Never shapen nor outlined:
From myself the fear has grown,
And the shadow is my own.
Yet, O Lord, through all a sense
Of Thy tender providence
Stays my falling heart on Thee,
And confirms the feeble knee;
And, at times, my worn feet press
Spaces of cool quietness,
Lilied whiteness shone upon
Not by light of moon or sun.

Hours there be of inmost calm,
Broken but by grateful psalm,
When I love Thee more than fear Thee,
And Thy blessed Christ seems near me,
With forgiving look, as when
He beheld the Magdalen.
Well I know that all things move
To the spheral rhythm of love,—
That to Thee, O Lord of all!

John Greenleaf Whittier

95

From *Lovest Thou Me?*

Lord it is my chief complaint,
That my love is weak and faint;
Yet I love Thee and adore,—
Oh! for grace to love Thee more!

William Cowper

96

From *The Approach*

O Lord, I wonder at thy Lov
Which did my Infancy so early mov:
But more at that which did forbear
And mov'd so long, tho slighted many a Year:
But most of all, O God, that thou
Shouldst me at last convert I scarce know how.

Thy Gracious Motions oft in vain
Assaulted me: My Heart did hard remain
Long time: I sent my God away
Much griev'd y^t^ He could not impart His Joy.
I careless was, nor did regard
The End for which He all these Thoughts prepar'd.

But now with new & open Eys
I see beneath as if abov the Skies:

When I on what is past reflect
His Thoughts & Mine I plainly recollect;
He did approach me, nay, did woo;
I wonder that my God so much would do.

Thomas Traherne

97 From *Certaine Sonets*

Leave me o Love, which reachest but to dust,
And thou my mind aspire to higher things:
Grow rich in that which never taketh rust:
What ever fades, but fading pleasure brings.

Draw in thy beames, and humble all thy might,
To that sweet yoke, where lasting freedomes be:
Which breakes the clowdes and opens forth the light
That doth both shine and give us sight to see.

O take fast hold, let that light be thy guide,
In this small course which birth drawes out to death,
And thinke how evil becommeth him to slide,
Who seeketh heav'n, and comes of heav'nly breath.
Then farewell world, thy uttermost I see,
Eternall Love maintaine thy life in me.

Philip Sidney

98 *O Deus, Ego Amo Te*

O God, I love thee, I love thee—
Not out of hope of heaven for me
Nor fearing not to love and be
In the everlasting burning.
Thou, thou, my Jesus, after me
Didst reach thine arms out dying,
For my sake sufferedst nails and lance,
Mocked and marrèd countenance,

Sorrows passing number,
Sweat and care and cumber,
Yea and death, and this for me,
And thou couldst see me sinning:
Then I, why should not I love thee,
Jesu, so much in love with me?
Not for heaven's sake; not to be
Out of hell by loving thee;
Not for any gains I see;
But just the way that thou didst me
I do love and I will love thee:
What must I love thee, Lord, for then?
For being my king and God. Amen.

Gerard Manley Hopkins

99 *Prayer of St. Francis Xavier*

Thou art my God, sole object of my love;
Not for the hope of endless joys above;
Not for the fear of endless pains below,
Which they who love thee not must undergo.

For me, and such as me, thou deign'st to bear
An ignominious cross, the nails, the spear:
A thorny crown transpierc'd thy sacred brow,
While bloody sweats from ev'ry member flow.

For me in tortures thou resignd'st thy breath,
Embrac'd me on the cross, and sav'd me by thy death.
And can these sufferings fail my heart to move?
What but thyself can now deserve my love?

Such as then was, and is, thy love to me,
Such is, and shall be still, my love to thee—
To thee, Redeemer! mercy's sacred spring!
My God, my Father, Maker, and my King!

Alexander Pope

6 · IN WHOM IS FORGIVENESS

100 From *The Poet's Journal*

God, to whom we look up blindly,
Look Thou down upon us kindly:
We have sinned, but not designedly.

If our faith in Thee was shaken,
Pardon Thou our hearts mistaken,
Our obedience reawaken.

We are sinful, Thou art holy:
Thou art mighty, we are lowly:
Let us reach Thee, climbing slowly.

Our ingratitude confessing,
On Thy mercy still transgressing,
Thou dost punish us with blessing!

Bayard Taylor

101 *A Hymne to God the Father*

Wilt thou forgive that sinne where I begunne,
Which is my sin, though it were done before?
Wilt thou forgive those sinnes, through which I runne,
And do run still: though still I do deplore?
When thou hast done, thou hast not done,
For I have more.

Wilt thou forgive that sinne by which I have wonne
Others to sinne? and, made my sinne their doore?
Wilt thou forgive that sinne which I did shunne
A yeare, or two: but wallowed in, a score?

When thou hast done, thou hast not done,
For I have more.

I have a sinne of feare, that when I have spunne
My last thred, I shall perish on the shore;
Sweare by thy selfe, that at my death thy sonne
Shall shine as he shines now, and heretofore;
And, having done that, Thou haste done,
I feare no more.

John Donne

102

Mea Culpa

Be pitiful, my God!
No hard-won gifts I bring—
But empty, pleading hands
To Thee at evening.

Spring came, white-browed and young,
I, too, was young with Spring.
There was a blue, blue heaven
Above a skylark's wing.

Youth is the time for joy,
I cried, it is not meet
To mount the heights of toil
With child-soft feet.

When Summer walked the land
In Passion's red arrayed,
Under green sweeping boughs
My couch I made.

The noon-tide heat was sore,
I slept the Summer through;
An angel waked me—"Thou
Hast work to do."

I rose and saw the sheaves
  Upstanding in a row;
The reapers sang Thy praise
  While passing to and fro.

My hands were soft with ease,
  Long were the Autumn hours;
I left the ripened sheaves
  For poppy-flowers.

But lo! now Winter glooms,
  And gray is in my hair,
Whither has flown the world
  I found so fair?

My patient God, forgive!
  Praying Thy pardon sweet
I lay a lonely heart
  Before Thy feet.

Ethna Carbery

103 *Eternal Lord! Eased of a Cumbrous Load*

Eternal Lord! eased of a cumbrous load,
And loosened from the world, I turn to Thee;
Shun, like a shattered bark, the storm, and flee
To thy protection for a safe abode.
The crown of thorns, hands pierced upon the tree,
The meek, benign, and lacerated face,
To a sincere repentance promise grace,
To the sad soul give hope of pardon free.
With justice mark not Thou, O Light divine,
My fault, nor hear it with thy sacred ear;
Neither put forth that way thy arm severe;
Wash with thy blood my sins; thereto incline

More readily the more my years require
Help, and forgiveness speedy and entire.

Michelangelo Buonarroti
Tr. William Wordsworth

104 *A Last Prayer*

Father, I scarcely dare to pray,
  So clear I see, now it is done,
That I have wasted half my day,
  And left my work but just begun.

So clear I see that things I thought
  Were right or harmless were a sin;
So clear I see that I have sought,
  Unconscious, selfish aims to win;

So clear I see that I have hurt
  The souls I might have helped to save;
That I have slothful been, inert,
  Deaf to the calls thy leaders gave.

In outskirts of thy kingdom vast,
  Father, the humblest spot give me;
Set me the lowliest task thou hast;
  Let me repentant work for thee!

Helen Hunt Jackson

105 *A Prayer*

When I look back upon my life nigh spent,
  Nigh spent, although the stream as yet flows on,
I more of follies than of sins repent,
  Less for offence than Love's shortcomings moan,
  With self, O Father, leave me not alone—
Leave not with the beguiler the beguiled;

Besmirched and ragged, Lord, take back thine own:
A fool I bring thee to be made a child.

George Macdonald

106 From *The Fool's Prayer*

'Tis not by guilt the onward sweep
Of truth and right, O Lord, we stay;
'Tis by our follies that so long
We hold the earth from heaven away.

These clumsy feet, still in the mire,
Go crushing blossoms without end;
These hard, well-meaning hands we thrust
Among the heart-strings of a friend.

The ill-timed truth we might have kept—
Who knows how sharp it pierced and stung?
The word we had not sense to say—
Who knows how grandly it had rung?

Our faults no tenderness should ask,
The chastening stripes must cleanse them all;
But for our blunders—oh, in shame
Before the eyes of heaven we fall.

Edward Rowland Sill

107 *A Pagan Reinvokes the Twenty-Third Psalm*

I knock again and try the key,
I, who, enraged, fled from Thy temple's trees
Because the presence of my enemies
Around the table there offended me. . . .
I, who laid up so long and bitterly
Complaints and old reproaches, on my knees
Offer regret for years misspent as these,
And wonder how such folly came to be.

Anoint again my head and let me walk
The valley of the shadow, with the rod
Thou hast afforded for my comfort, God:
My soul restored, and singing through my veins.
Forgive the years of idle, foolish talk:
The cup that runneth over still remains.

Robert L. Wolf

108

Resolution

Love, You have struck me straight, my Lord!
  Past innocence, past guilt,
I carry in my soul the sword
  You buried to the hilt.

And though to eyes in terrible pain
  Heaven and earth may reel,
For fear You may not strike again
  I will not draw the steel.

Charles L. O'Donnell

109

Qui Laborat, Orat

O only Source of all our light and life,
  Whom as our truth, our strength, we see and feel,
But whom the hours of mortal moral strife
  Alone aright reveal!

Mine inmost soul, before Thee inly brought,
  Thy presence owns ineffable, divine;
Chastised each rebel self-encentered thought,
  My will adoreth Thine.

With eye down-dropt, if then this earthly mind
  Speechless remain, or speechless e'en depart;
Nor seek to see—for what of earthly kind
  Can see Thee as Thou art?—

If well-assured 'tis but profanely bold
  In thought's abstractest forms to seem to see,
It dare not dare the dread communion hold
  In ways unworthy Thee.

O not unowned, Thou shalt unnamed forgive,
  In worldly walks the prayerless heart prepare;
And if in work its life it seem to live,
  Shalt make that work be prayer.

Nor times shall lack, when while the work it plies,
  Unsummoned powers the blinding film shall part,
And scarce by happy tears made dim, the eyes
  In recognition start.

But, as thou willest, give or e'en forbear
  The beatific supersensual sight,
So, with Thy blessing blest, that humbler prayer
  Approach Thee morn and night.

Arthur Hugh Clough

110

For Deeper Life

Dear God our Father, at Thy knee confessing
  Our sins and follies, close in Thine embrace,
Children forgiven, happy in Thy blessing,
  Deepen our spirits to receive Thy grace.

Not for more beauty would our eyes entreat Thee,
  Flooded with beauty, beauty everywhere;
Only with keener vision that may greet Thee
  In all Thy vestures of the earth and air.

The stars and rainbows are Thy wondrous wearing,
  Sunlight and shadow moving on the hills;
Holy the meadow where Thy feet are faring,
  Holy the brooklet that Thy laughter fills.

Not for more love our craving hearts implore Thee,
  But for more power to love until they glow
Like hearths of comfort eager to restore Thee
  Hidden in human wretchedness and woe.

In souls most sullen Thou art softly dreaming
  Of saints and heroes wrought from Thy divine,
Pity and patience still the lost redeeming.
  Deepen our spirits for a love like Thine.

Katharine Lee Bates

111 *Prayer of the Young Stoic*

(Rome, Second Century A.D.*)*

Bodiless, nameless God,
Forgive me my mankind—
That I am not a clod
Or dust upon the wind.

Forgive me that I weep
For what you may not save,
Or strive to overleap
The black gap of the grave.

My shivering spirit shrinks
From cold, demanding glory
And, stooping earthward, drinks
From warm old wells of story.

Oh Universe, forgive
My folly, fear, and pain;
With thee I cannot live,
And turn from thee—in vain.

Stephen P. Dunn

7 · AS THOU WILT

112 From *The Return*

Father of Life, with songs of wonder,
I praise Thee, even to this end,
Love unto Thee all loves surrender,
From Whom they flow, towards Whom they tend.

Mine is Thy Will, I yield the spirit
Still on Thine errand without cease
Gladly to run, or to inherit
In Thine eternal dwelling peace.

Margaret L. Woods

113 *In Harbor*

If hungry, Lord, I need bread;
If I be faint, a cooling cup;
Naught, if I weary, save a bed;
If halt, a staff to hold me up;
If needy, fields to till:
Yet, Lord, I wait Thy will.

Lizette Woodworth Reese

114 From *A Heathen Hymn*

I praise Thee not, with impious pride,
For that Thy partial hand has given
Bounties of wealth or form or brain,
Good gifts to other men denied.

Nor weary Thee with blind request,
For fancied goods Thy hand withholds;

I know not what to fear or hope,
Nor aught but that Thy will is best.

Lewis Morris

115 *Lord! Who Art Merciful as Well as Just*

Lord! who art merciful as well as just,
Incline thine ear to me, a child of dust:
Not what I would, O Lord! I offer thee,
  Alas! but what I can.
Father Almighty, who hast made me man,
And bade me look to heaven, for thou art there,
Accept my sacrifice and humble prayer.
Four things which are not in thy treasury,
I lay before thee, Lord, with this petition:—
  My nothingness, my wants,
  My sins, and my contrition.

Robert Southey

116 *O Martyred Spirit*

O martyred Spirit of this helpless Whole,
Who dost by pain for tyranny atone,
And in the star, the atom, and the stone,
Purgest the primal guilt, and in the soul;
Rich but in grief, thou dost thy wealth unroll,
And givest of thy substance to thine own,
Mingling the love, the laughter, and the groan
In the large hollow of the heaven's bowl.
Fill full my cup; the dregs and honeyed brim
I take from thy just hand, more worthy love
For sweetening not the draught for me or him.
What in myself I am, that let me prove;
Relent not for my feeble prayer, nor dim
The burning of thine altar for my hymn.

George Santayana

117 *View Mee, Lord*

View mee, Lord, a worke of thine:
Shall I then lye drown'd in night?
Might thy grace in mee but shine,
I should seeme made all of light.

But my soule still surfets so
On the poysoned baytes of sinne,
That I strange and vgly growe,
All is darke and foule within.

Clense mee, Lord, that I may kneele
At thine Altar, pure and white:
They that once thy Mercies feele,
Gaze no more on earths delight.

Worldly ioyes like shadowes fade,
When the heau'nly light appeares;
But the cou'nants thou hast made,
Endlesse, know nor days, nor yeares.

In thy word, Lord, is my trust,
To thy mercies fast I flye;
Though I am but clay and dust,
Yet thy grace can lift me high.

Thomas Campion

118 From *Pauline*

My God, my God, let me for once look on thee
As though naught else existed, we alone!
And as creation crumbles, my soul's spark
Expands till I can say,—Even from myself.
I need thee and I feel thee and I love thee.
I do not plead my rapture in thy works

For love of thee, nor that I feel as one
Who cannot die: but there is that in me
Which turns to thee, which loves or which should love.

Robert Browning

119 *O Thou Immortal Deity*

O Thou immortal deity
Whose throne is in the depth of human thought,
I do adjure thy power and thee
By all that man may be, by all that he is not,
By all that he has been and yet must be.

Percy Bysshe Shelley

120 *O Love That Wilt Not Let Me Go*

O Love that wilt not let me go,
I rest my weary soul in Thee;
I give Thee back the life I owe,
That in Thine ocean depths its flow
May richer, fuller be.

O Light that followest all my way,
I yield my flickering torch to Thee;
My heart restores its borrowed ray,
That in Thy sunshine's blaze its day
May brighter, fairer be.

O Joy that seekest me through pain,
I cannot close my heart to Thee;
I trace the rainbow through the rain,
And feel the promise is not vain
That morn shall tearless be.

O Cross that liftest up my head,
I dare not ask to fly from Thee;
I lay in dust life's glory dead,

And from the ground there blossoms red
    Life that shall endless be.

O Hope that lightenest all my way,
  I cannot choose but cleave to Thee,
And wrestle till the break of day
Disclose the wisdom of the way
    In blessings yet to be.

George Matheson

121 *Hymn of Trust*

O Love Divine, that stooped to share
  Our sharpest pang, our bitterest tear,
On Thee we cast each earth-born care,
  We smile at pain while Thou art near!

Though long the weary way we tread,
  And sorrow crown each lingering year,
No path we shun, no darkness dread,
  Our hearts still whispering, Thou art near!

When drooping pleasure turns to grief,
  And trembling faith is changed to fear,
The murmuring wind, the quivering leaf,
  Shall softly tell us, Thou art near!

On Thee we fling our burdening woe,
  O Love Divine, forever dear,
Content to suffer while we know,
  Living and dying, Thou art near!

Oliver Wendell Holmes

122 From *For the Time Being*

Our Father, whose creative Will
  Asked Being for us all,

Confirm it that Thy Primal Love
May weave in us the freedom of
The actually deficient on
  The justly actual.

Though written by Thy children with
  A smudged and crooked line,
The Word is ever legible,
Thy Meaning unequivocal,
And for Thy Goodness even sin
  Is valid as a sign.

Inflict Thy promises with each
  Occasion of distress,
That from our incohence we
May learn to put our trust in Thee,
And brutal fact persuade us to
  Adventure, Art, and Peace.

W. H. Auden

8 · OUR LIFE IN HIM

123 From *The Eternal Goodness*

And Thou, O Lord! by whom are seen
Thy creatures as they be,
Forgive me if too close I lean
My human heart on Thee!

John Greenleaf Whittier

124 *L'Envoi*

O love triumphant over guilt and sin,
My soul is soiled, but Thou shalt enter in;
My feet must stumble if I walk alone,
Lonely my heart, till beating by Thine own,
My will is weakness till it rest in Thine,
Cut off, I wither, thirsting for the Vine,
My deeds are dry leaves on a sapless tree,
My life is lifeless till it live in Thee!

Frederic Lawrence Knowles

125 *Hymn*

When storms arise
And dark'ning skies
About me threat'ning lower,
To thee, O Lord, I raise mine eyes,
To thee my tortured spirit flies
For solace in that hour.

The mighty arm
Will let no harm
Come near me nor befall me;

Thy voice shall quiet my alarm,
When life's great battle waxeth warm—
No foeman shall apall me.

Upon thy breast
Secure I rest,
From sorrow and vexation;
No more my sinful cares oppressed,
But in thy presence ever blest,
O God of my salvation.

Paul Laurence Dunbar

126 *O Thou Whose Image*

O thou whose image in the shrine
Of human spirits dwells divine;
Which from that precinct once conveyed,
To be to outer day displayed,
Doth vanish, part, and leave behind
Mere blank and void of empty mind,
Which wilful fancy seeks in vain
With casual shapes to fill again—

O thou that in our bosoms' shrine
Dost dwell, because unknown, divine!
I thought to speak, I thought to say,
'The light is here,' 'behold the way,'
'The voice was thus,' and 'thus the word,'
And 'thus I saw,' and 'that I hear,'—
But from the lips but half essayed
The imperfect utterance fell unmade.

O thou, in that mysterious shrine
Enthroned, as we must say, divine!
I will not frame one thought of what
Thou mayest either be or not.

I will not prate of 'thus' and 'so,'
And be profane with 'yes' and 'no.'
Enough that in our soul and heart
Thou, whatsoe'er thou may'st be, art.

Unseen, secure in that high shrine
Acknowledged present and divine,
I will not ask some upper air,
Some future day, to place thee there;
Nor say, nor yet deny, Such men
Or women saw thee thus and then:
Thy name was such, and there or here
To him or her thou didst appear.

Do only thou in that dim shrine,
Unknown or known, remain, divine;
There, or if not, at least in eyes
That scan the fact that round them lies.
The hand to sway, the judgment guide,
In sight and sense thyself divide:
Be thou but there,—in soul and heart,
I will not ask to feel thou art.

Arthur Hugh Clough

127 From *Happiness Found*

Lord, it is not Life to live,
   If thy Presence thou deny:
Lord, if thou thy Presence give,
   'Tis no longer Death to die:
Source and Giver of Repose,
Singly from thy Smile it flows;
Peace and Happiness are thine;
Mine they are, if Thou art mine.

Whilst I feel thy Love to me,
   Ev'ry object teems with Joy,

Here, O may I walk with Thee,
  Then into thy Presence Die!
Let me but Thyself possess,
Total Sum of Happiness!
Real Bliss I then shall prove;
Heav'n below, and Heav'n above.

Augustus M. Toplady

128 *An Hymn on the Omnipresence*

Oh Lord! thou hast known me, and searched me out,
Thou see'st, at all Times, what I'm thinking about;
When I rise up to Labour, or lye down to Rest,
Thou markest each Motion that works in my Breast;
My Heart has no Secrets, but what thou can'st tell,
Not a Word in my Tongue, but thou knowest it well;
Thou see'st my Intention before it is wrought,
Long before I conceive it, thou knowest my Thought.

Thou art always about me, go whither I will,
All the Paths that I take to, I meet with thee still;
I go forth abroad, and am under thine Eye,
I retire to myself, and behold! thou art by;
How is it that thou hast encompass'd me so
That I cannot escape thee, wherever I go?
Such Knowledge as this is too high to attain,
'Tis a Truth which I feel, tho' I cannot explain.

Whither then shall I flee from thy Spirit, O Lord?
What Shelter can Space from thy Presence afford?
If I climb up to Heav'n, 'tis there is thy Throne,
If I go down to Hell, even there thou art known;
If for Wings I should mount on the Mornings swift Ray,
And remain in the uttermost Parts of the Sea,
Even there, let the Distance be ever so wide,
Thy Hand would support me, thy right Hand would guide.

If I say, peradventure, the Dark may conceal
What Distance, tho' boundless, is forc'd to reveal,
Yet the Dark, at thy Presence, would vanish away,
And my Covering, the Night, would be turn'd into Day:
It is I myself only who could not then see,
Yea, the Darkness, O Lord, is no Darkness to Thee:
The Night, and the Day, are alike in thy Sight,
And the Darkness, to Thee, is as clear as the Light.

John Byrom

129 *Unseen*

Thou great Supreme, whom angel choirs adore,
High over all exalted evermore,
No mortal eye hath seen at any time
The matchless glory of Thy throne sublime;
Yet unto us Thou dost Thyself reveal;
Within our souls Thy presence, Lord, we feel,
And know that we from death to life have passed,
That with Thy chosen ones our lot is cast.

Unseen, yet when in prayer we breathe Thy name,
Our love inspired is kindled to a flame;
Till, upward borne on eagle wings, we soar
Beyond the clouds that veil the eternal shore,
And view by faith Thy regal diadem,
And in a vision touch Thy garment's hem.

Unseen, Thou lead'st us by Thine own right hand;
Thus saith Thy word, upon whose truth we stand;
And still again we hear in tones divine,
"Fear not; I have redeemed you; ye are mine."

Unseen, but O how precious, Lord, Thou art!
How sweet Thy voice to every trusting heart!
We praise and bless Thee for the promise given

Of endless joy and perfect rest in Heaven,
Where, Thou hast said, through Thy abundant grace,
We shall in righteousness behold Thy face.

Fanny Crosby

130 *Depart From Me*

Depart from me. I know Thee not!
  Within the Temple have I sought Thee,
  And many a time have sold and bought Thee
In that unhallowed, holy spot.
Depart from me. I know Thee not!

Depart from me. I know Thee not!
  Full oft among the poor I found Thee.
  There did I grieve, neglect, and wound Thee.
I never strove to share Thy lot.
Depart from me. I know Thee not!

I know Thee not. Abide with me!
  More than aught else do I admire Thee,
  Above all earthly things desire Thee.
I am Thy prisoner. Make me free!
I know Thee not. Abide with me!

Mary Elizabeth Coleridge

131 *Hymn*

Since without Thee we do no good,
  And with Thee do no ill,
Abide with us in weal and woe,—
  In action and in will.

In weal,—that, while our lips confess
  The Lord who "gives," we may
Remember, with an humble thought,
  The Lord who "takes away."

In woe,—that, while to drowning tears
  Our hearts their joys resign,
We may remember *who* can turn
  Such water into wine.

By hours of day,—that, when our feet
  O'er hill and valley run,
We still may think the light of truth
  More welcome than the sun.

By hours of night,—that, when the air
  Its dew and shadow yields,
We still may hear the voice of God
  In silence of the fields.

Oh! then sleep comes on us like death,
  All soundless, deaf and deep:
Lord! teach us so to watch and pray,
  That death may come like sleep.

Abide with *us*, abide with *us*,
  While flesh and soul agree;
And when our flesh is only dust,
  Abide our souls with *Thee*.

Elizabeth Barrett Browning

132

Man

My God, I heard this day,
That none doth build a stately habitation,
  But he that means to dwell therein.
  What house more stately hath there been,
Or can be, then is Man? to whose creation
    All things are in decay.

❋

  Since then, my God, thou hast
So brave a Palace built; O dwell in it,

That it may dwell with thee at last!
Till then, afford us so much wit;
That, as the world serves us, we may serve thee,
And both thy servants be.

George Herbert

133 *Come Down*

Still am I haunting
Thy door with my prayers;
Still they are panting
Up thy steep stairs!
Wouldst thou not rather
Come down to my heart,
And there, O my Father,
Be what thou art?

George Macdonald

134 *The Prayer*

Wilt Thou not visit me?
The plant beside me feels thy gentle dew,
And every blade of grass I see
From thy deep earth its quickening moisture drew.

Wilt Thou not visit me?
Thy morning calls on me with cheering tone;
And every hill and tree
Lend but one voice,—the voice of Thee alone.

Come, for I need thy love,
More than the flower the dew or grass the rain;
Come, gently as thy holy dove;
And let me in thy sight rejoice to live again.

I will not hide from them
When thy storms come, though fierce may be their wrath,

But how with leafy stem,
And strengthened follow on thy chosen path.

Yes, Thou wilt visit me:
Nor plant nor tree thine eye delights so well,
As, when from sin set free,
My spirit loves with thine in peace to dwell.

Jones Very

135 *Requests*

I asked for Peace—
My sins arose,
And bound me close,
I could not find release.

I asked for Truth—
My doubts came in,
And with their din
They wearied all my youth.

I asked for Love—
My lovers failed,
And griefs assailed
Around, beneath, above.

I asked for Thee—
And Thou didst come
To take me home
Within Thy Heart to be.

Digby Mackworth Dolben

136 *Prayer for Peace*

Attack me, Father, now,
As when the sea

Rushes the rising rocks
   Relentlessly.

Then, with the easing done,
   Gather increase,
Circle my stubborn soul,
   Lap it in peace.

Johnstone G. Patrick

137 *The Mirror*

Lord, make my soul
To mirror Thee,
Thyself alone
To shine in me,
That men may see
Thy love, Thy grace,
Nor note the glass
That shows Thy Face.

Blanche Mary Kelly

138 *The Mystic's Prayer*

Lay me to sleep in sheltering flame
   O Master of the Hidden Fire!
Wash pure my heart, and cleanse for me
   My soul's desire.

In flame of sunrise bathe my mind,
   O Master of the Hidden Fire,
That, when I wake, clear-eyed may be
   My soul's desire.

William Sharp

139 *Plea for Hope*

O Morning-Maker, deign that ray
Of alien star may sheen our day

Whereof the sun but darkens sight
In quest of mere, unfashioned Light!

Set Thou on high a twinkling hope
To lead us up from glen to slope;
From mastered peak to humbled crest,
And so through heavens Thy mercy blessed,

When shone the East from Paradise
On Asian blues of miraged skies
Which, manifesting Orient Fire,
Left John horizoned of desire:

That inly seen, that showing forth
Of Beauty's Heaven to gaping earth,
The which so far transcended, Lord,
The Son of Thunder's trembling word;

Yea, shunned his soul-experience till,
As part of Thy Invisible,
He lost that hope which, having gained,
We too would lose in Thee attained.

Francis Carlin

140 *A Song*

Lord, when the sense of Thy sweet grace
Sends up my soul to seek Thy face,
Thy blessed eyes breed such desire
I die in Love's delicious fire.
  O Love, I am Thy sacrifice!
Be still triumphant, blessed eyes!
Still shine on me, fair suns! that I
Still may behold, though still I die.

Though still I die, I live again,
Still longing so to be still slain;

So gainful is such loss of breath,
I die even in desire of death.
  Still live in me this loving strife
Of living death and dying life;
For while Thou sweetly slayest me,
Dead to myself, I live in Thee.

Richard Crashaw

141 ## *Prayer*

The invisible world with thee hath sympathized;
Be thy affections raised and solemnized.
Wordsworth, "Laodamia"

Omnipotent confederate of all good,
Inexorable foe of all our ill,
Extirpate these bold motions of self-will,
Mortify these strange slips, the unblushing brood
Of vanities, and be thy surgery rude,
Until we wake to thee alone, until
All mild and disabused and meek and still
We pass in awe into thy plenitude.
So in an hour we have seen the face
Of nature change, and with our garish eyes
As though anointed with some lymph of grace
Seen common day grow solemn, as the skies
Foaming above with sable panoplies
Made of the world a hushed transfigured place.

Amos N. Wilder

142 ## *Hymn*

Great Spirit of the speeding spheres,
Whose constant orbits mark the years,
Whose tides arise, then flow apart,
As pulse-beats of the cosmic heart;

Thou God to whom an aeon gone
Is but as yesterday when done,
The centuries' march of tribe and clan
The shadow of a moment's span;

How canst Thou know our transient days?
Why shouldst Thou trace our trivial ways?
Why hold within Thine awful hand
These motes of dust, these grains of sand?

Yet we are Thine! The eternal flood
Flows through the currents of our blood,
The undying fire of star and sun
Kindles our souls, and makes them one.

One with Thy life, ere time began,
Nor knew the rise and fall of man;
One till the numbered years are fled,
And earth to cold and darkness sped!

Teach us, O God, the purpose high
Which moves the spaces of the sky,
That our quick day, from error free,
May live in Thine eternity.

John Haynes Holmes

143 *A Seaman's Confession of Faith*

As long as I go forth on ships that sail
The mighty seas, my faith, O Lord, won't fail;
And while the stars march onward mightily
In white, great hosts, I shall remember Thee;
I have seen men one moment all alive,
The next, gone out with none to bless or shrive
Into the unseen place where all must go,—
So, Lord, thy mercy and thy gifts I know. . . .
They think me Godless, maybe, but indeed

They do not see how I have read thy creed
In flowing tides and waves that heave and run
Beyond the endless west where sinks the sun;
In the long, long night-watches I have thought
On things that neither can be sold nor bought,
Rare, priceless things; nor have I scorned nor
scoffed
At thy sure might, when lost in storms aloft:
The prayer and faith of seamen will not fail
O God, my God, as long as ships do sail.

Harry Kemp

III

THOU CRYSTAL CHRIST

1 · IN HIM WAS LIFE

144 From *The Crystal*

But Thee, but Thee, O sovereign Seer of time,
But Thee, O poets' Poet, Wisdom's Tongue,
But Thee, O man's best Man, O love's best Love,
O perfect life in perfect labor writ,
O all men's Comrade, Servant, King, or Priest,—
What *if* or *yet*, what mole, what flaw, what lapse,
What least defect or shadow of defect,
What rumor, tattled by an enemy,
Of inference loose, what lack of grace
Even in torture's grasp, or sleep's, or death's,—
Oh, what amiss may I forgive in Thee,
Jesus, good Paragon, thou Crystal Christ?

Sidney Lanier

145 *A Morning Hymn*

What's this Morns bright Eye to Me,
If I see not thine, & Thee,
Fairer Jesu; in whose Face
All my Heavn is spred! Alas,
Still I grovel in dead Night,
Whilst I want thy living Light;
Dreaming with wide open eyes,
Fond fantastick Vanities.
  Shine, my onely Daystarr, shine:
So mine Eyes shall wake by Thine;
So the Dreams I grope in now
To clear Visions shall grow;
So my Day shall measured be
By thy Graces claritie;

So shall I discern the Path
Thy sweet law prescribed hath;
For thy Wayes cannot be shown
By any Light, but by *thine own.*

Joseph Beaumont

146 *A Morning Hymn*

Christ, whose Glory fills the Skies,
  Christ, the true, the only Light,
Sun of Righteousness, arise,
  Triumph o'er the Shades of Night:
Day-spring from on High, be near:
Day-star, in my Heart appear.

Dark and Chearless is the Morn
  Unaccompanied by Thee,
Joyless is the Day's Return,
  Till thy Mercy's Beams I see;
Till they Inward Light impart,
Glad my Eyes, and warm my Heart.

Visit then this Soul of mine,
  Pierce the Gloom of Sin, and Grief,
Fill me, Radiancy Divine,
  Scatter all my Unbelief,
More and more Thyself display,
Shining to the Perfect Day.

Charles Wesley

147 *A Psalm to the Son*

Suddenly, out of my darkness, shines Thy beauty, O Brother;
  Brother, the light of Thy life is a blessing beyond all brightness.
I am smitten blind and see the pride of the world no longer;
  I am smitten with new light that shows the glory of love.
Thy way is more wonderful than the way of the sun at noon,

For wherever Thy light falls it cleanses us from evil;
Thy way is more beautiful than the way of the moon in the evening,
For wherever Thy light falls it is healing for our pain;
Thy way is dearer by far than the way of the little stars,
For wherever Thy light falls it is leading us to peace;
Thy way is holier than ever the sinful lips of man can tell,
Thy glory is yet to burn in the hearts of all mankind.
I, who would sing Thy beauty, have known the darkness, Brother.
Oh, wash my eyes with tears that they may know the light of Thy love!

Marguerite Wilkinson

148 *Thou Light of Ages*

Thou Light of Ages, Source of living truth,
Shine into every groping, seeking mind;
Let plodding age and pioneering youth
Each day some clearer, brighter pathway find.

Thou Light of Ages, shining forth in Christ,
Whose brightness darkest ages could not dim,
Grant us the spirit which for Him sufficed—
Rekindle here the torch of love for Him.

Rolland W. Schloerb

149 From *The Name of Jesus*

Jesus! my Shepherd, Husband, Friend,
My Prophet, Priest, and King;
My Lord, my Life, my Way, my End,
Accept the praise I bring.

Weak is the effort of my heart,
And cold my warmest thought;
But when I see thee as thou art,
I'll praise thee as I ought.

'Till then I would thy love proclaim
  With ev'ry fleeting breath;
And may the music of thy name
  Refresh my soul in death.

John Newton

150 *O Thou Who Camest from Above*

O Thou who camest from above,
  The pure, celestial fire t' impart,
Kindle a flame of sacred love
  On the mean altar of my heart;
There let it for thy glory burn
  With inextinguishable blaze,
And trembling to it's Source return,
  In humble prayer, and fervent praise.

Jesus, confirm my heart's desire
  To work, and speak, and think for thee,
Still let me guard the holy fire,
  And still stir up thy gift in me,
Ready for all thy perfect will
  My acts of faith and love repeat,
'Till death thy endless mercies seal,
  And make my sacrifice compleat.

Charles Wesley

2 · HIS COMING

151 *That Holy Thing*

They all were looking for a king
  To slay their foes, and lift them high:
Thou cam'st a little baby thing
  That made a woman cry.

O son of man, to right my lot
  Nought but thy presence can avail;
Yet on the road thy wheels are not,
  Nor on the sea thy sail!

My fancied ways why shouldst thou heed?
  Thou com'st down thine own secret stair;
Com'st down to answer all my need,
  Yea, every bygone prayer!

George Macdonald

152 *To the Child Jesus*

I

The Nativity

Could every time-worn heart but see Thee once again,
A happy human child, among the homes of men,
The age of doubt would pass,—the vision of Thy face
Would silently restore the childhood of the race.

II

The Flight into Egypt

Thou wayfaring Jesus, a pilgrim and stranger,
  Exiled from heaven by love at thy birth,

Exiled again from thy rest in the manger,
  A fugitive child 'mid the perils of earth,—
Cheer with thy fellowship all who are weary,
  Wandering far from the land that they love;
Guide every heart that is homeless and dreary,
  Safe to its home in thy presence above.

Henry van Dyke

153 *All Hail, Thou Noble Guest*

All hail, Thou noble Guest, this morn,
Whose love did not the sinner scorn;
In my distress Thou com'st to me;
What thanks shall I return to Thee?

❊

Were earth a thousand times as fair,
Beset with gold and jewels rare,
She yet were far too poor to be,
A narrow cradle, Lord, for Thee.

❊

Ah dearest Jesus, Holy Child,
Make Thee a bed, soft, undefiled,
Within my heart, that it may be
A quiet chamber kept for Thee.

Martin Luther
Tr. by Arthur Tozer Russell
and Catherine Winkworth

154 *In Time of Need*

Never we needed Thee so sore
  Since the first day began,
O, come and knock at the world's door,
  Small Son of God and Man!
And if it ope not to Thy knock
  Shrill crying in the cold,

Break down the heart hard as a rock
  And enter and lay hold!

Not when they slew our young, and marred
  The beauty, smooth and clean,
Not then, not then, our hearts were hard,
  Arid and cold and mean.
For now the weak are down, and Hate,
  And Avarice, and Pride,
These are the Lords within our gate,
  O Child, be not denied!

O, not in nineteen hundred years
  We needed Thee as tonight.
Yest're'en we washed us clean with tears,
  Their scarlet washed us white,
There is not one green spot on earth
  Where men nor hate nor grieve.
O Child, come to our hour of dearth
  And bid the dead heart live.

Katharine Tynan Hinkson

155

From *Christmas 1898*

'Tis nigh two thousand years,
Since came the Prince of Peace,
Return Thou, calm our fears,
Make strife and war to cease;
Thick clouds to-day of doubt,
Obscure our faithful sight.
Shine, Blessed Sun, shine out,
The storms of Passion still,
Again, oh hidden will,
The wintry Earth fulfil
With Peace and Light!

Lewis Morris

156 From *Christmas Antiphones*

Thou whose birth on earth
  Angels sang to men,
While thy stars made mirth,
Saviour, at thy birth,
  This day born again;

As this night was bright
  With thy cradle-ray,
Very light of light,
Turn the wild world's night
  To thy perfect day.

❉

Thou the Word and Lord
  In all time and space
Heard, beheld, adored,
With all ages poured
  Forth before thy face,—

Lord, what worth in earth
  Drew thee down to die?
What therein was worth,
Lord, thy death and birth?
  What beneath thy sky?

Light above all love
  By thy love was lit,
And brought down the Dove
Feathered from above
  With the wings of it.

❉

Thou whose face gives grace
  As the sun's doth heat,
Let thy sun-bright face

Lighten time and space
  Here beneath thy feet.

Bid our peace increase,
  Thou that madest morn;
Bid oppressions cease;
Bid the night be peace;
  Bid the day be born.

Algernon Charles Swinburne

157 *Homo Factus Est*

Come to me, Belovèd,
  Babe of Bethlehem;
Lay aside Thy Sceptre
  And Thy Diadem.

Come to me, Belovèd;
  Light and healing bring;
Hide my sin and sorrow
  Underneath Thy wing.

Bid all fear and doubting
  From my soul depart,
As I feel the beating
  Of Thy Human Heart.

Look upon me sweetly
  With Thy Human Eyes
With Thy Human Finger
  Point me to the skies.

Safe from earthly scandal
  My poor spirit hide
In the utter stillness
  Of Thy wounded Side.

Guide me, ever guide me,
  With Thy piercèd Hand,
Till I reach the borders
  Of the pleasant land.

Then, my own Belovèd,
  Take me home to rest;
Whisper words of comfort;
  Lay me on Thy Breast.

Show me not the Glory
  Round about Thy Throne;
Show me not the flashes
  Of Thy jewelled Crown.

Hide me from the pity
  Of the Angels' Band,
Who ever sing Thy praises,
  And before Thee stand.

Hide me from the glances
  Of the Seraphin,—
They, so pure and spotless,
  I, so stained with sin.

Hide me from S. Michael
  With his flaming sword:—
Thou can'st understand me,
  O my Human Lord!

Jesu, my Belovèd,
  Come to me alone;
In Thy sweet embraces
  Make me all Thine own.

By the quiet waters,
  Sweetest Jesu, lead;

'Mid the virgin lilies,
  Purest Jesu, feed.

Only Thee, Belovèd,
  Only Thee, I seek.
Thou, the Man Christ Jesus,
  Strength in flesh made weak.
Digby Mackworth Dolben

158 *Dedication*

Holy Jesus, Thou art born
For my sake on Christmas morn.
Lord, as Thou art born for me,
I am born again to Thee.

Through the city and abroad,
Thou dost lead me unto God.
Wheresoe'er Thou leadest me,
Master, I will follow Thee.

To Thy love my love I give,
Thou dost die that I may live.
As Thou giv'st Thy life for me,
Lord, I give my life to Thee.

From the tomb I see Thee rise,
When the morning fills the skies.
Lord, as Thou art risen for me,
I will rise from death to Thee.
Victoria Saffelle Johnson

159 From *Royal Presents*

Instead of Incense (Blessed Lord) if wee
Can send a sigh or fervent Prayre to thee,

Instead of Myrrh if wee can but prouide
Teares that from paenitentiall eyes do slide
And though wee haue no Gold; if for our part
Wee can present thee with a broken heart
Thou wilt accept: & say those Easterne kings
Did not present thee with more precious things.

Nathaniel Wanley

160 *Hora Christi*

Sweet is the time for joyous folk
  Of gifts and minstrelsy;
Yet I, O lowly-hearted One,
  Crave but Thy company.
On lonesome road, beset with dread,
  My questing lies afar.
I have no light, save in the east
  The gleaming of Thy star.

In cloistered aisles they keep to-day
  Thy feast, O living Lord!
With pomp of banner, pride of song,
  And stately sounding word.
Mute stand the kings of power and place,
  While priests of holy mind
Dispense Thy blessed heritage
  Of peace to all mankind.

I know a spot where budless twigs
  Are bare above the snow,
And where sweet winter-loving birds
  Flit softly to and fro;
There with the sun for altar-fire,
  The earth for kneeling-place,
The gentle air for chorister,
  Will I adore Thy face.

Lord, underneath the great blue sky,
  My heart shall paean sing,
The gold and myrrh of meekest love
  Mine only offering.
Bliss of Thy birth shall quicken me;
  And for Thy pain and dole
Tears are but vain, so I will keep
  The silence of the soul.

Alice Brown

3 · THE DIVINE COMPANION

161 *The Dwelling-Place*

John 1:38–39

What happy, secret fountain,
Fair shade, or mountain,
Whose undiscover'd virgin glory
Boasts it this day, though not in story,
Was then Thy dwelling? did some cloud,
Fix'd to a tent, descend and shroud
My distress'd Lord? or did a star,
Beckon'd by Thee, though high and far,
In sparkling smiles haste gladly down
To lodge light, and increase her own?
My dear, dear God! I do not know
What lodg'd Thee then, nor where, nor how;
But I am sure Thou dost now come
Oft to a narrow, homely room,
Where Thou too hast put the least part;
My God, I mean my sinful heart.

Henry Vaughan

162 *O Christ, Thou Art Within Me Like a Sea*

O Christ, thou art within me like a sea,
Filling me as a slowly rising tide.
No rock or stone or sandbar may abide
Safe from thy coming and undrowned in thee.

Thou dost not break me by the might of storm,
But with a calm upsurging from the deep

Thou shuttest me in thy eternal keep
Where is no ebb, for fullness is thy norm.

And never is thy flood of life withdrawn;
Thou holdest me till I am all thy own.
This gradual overcoming is foreknown.
Thou art within me like a sea at dawn.

Edith Lovejoy Pierce

163 *Wanderers*

Our feet have wandered from thy path,
  Thou lowly Christ of Galilee,
Sweet prophet of the helping hand,
  Meek Lord of love and sympathy.

Thy faith was but to walk with God
  With humble heart and open mind,
But we have builded shrines of stone
  In which to worship—spirit-blind!

We lift our heads in loveless prayers,
  We glory in our well wrought creed,
Though righteousness alone avails,
  Though mercy is the only need.

Break down, O Christ, our heartless faiths,
  And give to us that spirit fine
Which feels in thee a Comrade strong,
  In every soul a friend of thine.

Thomas Curtis Clark

164 From *Credo*

Christ of Judea, look thou in my heart!
Do I not love thee, look to thee, in thee

Alone have faith of all the sons of men—
Faith deepening with the weight and woe of years.

Pure soul and tenderest of all that came
Into this world of sorrow, hear my prayer:

Lead me, yea, lead me deeper into life,
This suffering, human life wherein thou liv'st
And breathest still, and hold'st thy way divine.
'T is here, O pitying Christ, where thee I seek,
Here where the strife is fiercest; where the sun
Beats down upon the highway thronged with men,
And in the raging mart. O! deeper lead
My soul into the living world of souls
Where thou dost move.

But lead me, Man Divine,
Where'er thou will'st, only that I may find
At the long journey's end thy image there,
And grow more like to it. For art not thou
The human shadow of the infinite Love
That made and fills the endless universe!
The very Word of Him, the unseen, unknown
Eternal Good that rules the summer flower
And all the worlds that people starry space!

Richard Watson Gilder

165 *To Jesus of Nazareth*

Closest to men, thou pitying Son of Man,
And thrilled from crown to foot with fellowship,
Yet most apart and strange, lonely as God,—
Dwell in my heart, remote and intimate One!
Brother of all the world, I come to Thee!

Gentle as she who nursed Thee at her breast
(Yet what a lash of lightnings once Thy tongue

To scourge the hypocrite and Pharisee!)—
Nerve Thou mine arm, O meek, O mighty One!
Champion of all who fail, I fly to Thee!

O man of sorrows, with the wounded hands,—
For chaplet, thorns; for throne, a pagan cross;
Bowed with the woe and agony of time,
Yet loved by children and the feasting guests,—
I bring my suffering, joyful heart to Thee.

Chaste as the virginal lily on her stem,
Yet in each hot, full pulse, each tropic vein,
More filled with feeling than the flow'r with sun;
No anchorite,—hale, sinewy, warm with love,—
I come in youth's tide of bliss to Thee.

O Christ of contrasts, infinite paradox,
Yet life's explainer, solvent harmony,
Frail strength, pure passion, meek austerity,
And the white splendor of these darken'd years,—
I lean my wondering, wayward heart on Thine.

Frederic Lawrence Knowles

166 *The Hem of His Garment*

O God of Calvary and Bethlehem,
Thou who did'st suffer rather than condemn,
Grant me to touch Thy garment's healing hem!

Thou trailest Thy fair robes of seamless light
Through this dark world of misery and night;
Its blackness cannot mar Thy spotless white.

Thou dost not, Master, as we pass Thee by,
Draw in Thy robes lest we should come too nigh;
We see no scorn in Thine all-sinless eye.

There is no shrinking even from our touch;
Thy tenderness to us is ever such,
It can endure and suffer much.

Anna Elizabeth Hamilton

167 *Savior! I've No One Else to Tell*

Savior! I've no one else to tell
And so I trouble Thee,
I am the one forgot Thee so.
Dost Thou remember me?

Not for myself I came so far,
That were the little load—
I brought Thee the imperial heart
I had not strength to hold.

The heart I carried in my own,
Till mine too heavy be,
Yet strangest—*heavier*
Since it went—
Is it too large for Thee?

Emily Dickinson

168 *The Prince of Life*

O Prince of Life, Thy Life hath tuned
All life to sweeter, loftier grace!
Life's common rounds have wider bounds,
Since Thou hast trod life's common ways.

O, Heart of Love! Thy Tenderness
Still runs through life's remotest vein;
And lust and greed and soulless creed
Shall never rule the world again.

O Life of Love!—The Good Intent
Of God to man made evident,—
All down the years, despite men's fears,
Thy Power is still omnipotent.

O Life! O Love! O Living Word!—
Rent Veil, revealing God to man,—
Help, Lord! Lest I should crucify,
By thought or deed, Thy Love again.

John Oxenham

169 *E Tenebris*

Come down, O Christ, and help me! reach thy hand
For I am drowning in a stormier sea
Than Simon on the lake of Galilee:
The wine of life is spilt upon the sand,
My heart is as some famine-murdered land
Whence all good things have perished utterly,
And well I know my soul in Hell must lie
If I this night before God's throne should stand.
"He sleeps perchance, or rideth to the chase,
Like Baal, when his prophets howled that name
From morn to noon on Carmel's smitten height."
Nay, peace, I shall behold, before the night,
The feet of brass, the robe more white than flame,
The wounded hands, the weary human face.

Oscar Wilde

4 · HIS DEATH AND TRIUMPH

170 *The Mediator*

How high Thou art! our songs can own
No music Thou couldst stoop to hear!
But still the Son's expiring groan
Is vocal in the Father's ear.

How pure Thou art! our hands are dyed
With curses, red with murder's hue—
But He hath stretched His hands to hide
The sins that pierced them from Thy view.

How strong Thou art! we tremble lest
The thunders of Thine arm be moved—
But He is lying on Thy breast,
And Thou must clasp Thy best Beloved!

How kind Thou art! Thou didst not choose
To joy in Him forever so;
But that embrace Thou wilt not lose
For vengeance, didst for love forego!

High God, and pure, and strong, and kind!
The low, the foul, the feeble, spare!
Thy brightness in His face we find—
Behold our darkness only *there!*

Elizabeth Barrett Browning

171 *Faith's Difficulty*

Not these appal
The soul tip-toeing to belief:

The ribald call,
The last black anguish of the thief;

The fellowship
Of publican and Pharisee,
The harlot's lip
Passionate with humility;

Or the feet kissed
By her who was the Magdalen—
The sensualist
Is one among a world of men!

Oh, I can look
Upon another's drama; read
As in a book
Things unrelated to my need;

Give faith's assent
To the abysmal love outpoured—
But why was rent
Thy seamless coat for *me,* dear Lord?

Why didst Thou bow
Thy bleeding brows for *my* heart's good?
How shall I now
Reach to the mystic hardihood

Where I can take
For personal treasure all Thy loss,
When for my sake,
My sake, Thou didst endure the cross?

For my soul's worth
Was "It is finished!" loudly cried?
For me the birth,
The sorrows of the crucified?

Theodore Maynard

172 *Stigmata*

In the wrath of the lips that assail us,
  In the scorn of the lips that are dumb,
The symbols of sorrow avail us,
  The joy of the people is come.
They parted Thy garments for barter,
  They follow Thy steps with complaint;
Let them know that the pyre of the martyr
  But purges the blood of the saint!

They have crucified Thee for a token;
  For a token Thy flesh crucified
Shall bleed in a heart that is broken
  For love of the wound in Thy side:
In pity for palms that were pleading,
  For feet that were grievously used,
There is blood on the brow that is bleeding
  And torn, as Thy brow that was bruised!

By Thee have we life, breath, and being;
  Thou hast knowledge of us and our kind;
Thou hast pleasure of eyes that are seeing,
  And sorrow of eyes that are blind;
By the seal of the mystery shown us—
  The wound that with Thy wounds accord—
O Lord, have mercy upon us!
  Have mercy upon us, O Lord!

Charles Warren Stoddard

173 *O Christ, Who Died*

O Christ, who died upon a cross,
My soul attests your sharpest pain:
'Twas not the spikes in hands or feet,
'Twas not the spearthrust in your side;

These were but instruments of death,
From which your spirit never winced.
No, Lord, the sword that thrust you through
Was in the hands of faithless friends;
Their gross indifference to your fate
Was sharper than the keenest blade.
To know that those you trusted most
Had failed you in your darkest hour—
This was the stroke that pierced your heart
And brought release to death's grim power.

O Christ, whose cross is ever new,
Alas, it must be so today,
As friends of yours still stand apart
And let you die with bleeding heart.

John Calvin Slemp

174 *A Hymne to God the Father*

Heare mee, O God!
A broken heart
Is my best part:
Use still thy rod,
That I may prove
Therein, thy Love.

If thou hadst not
Beene sterne to mee,
But left me free,
I had forgot
My selfe and thee.

For, sin's so sweet,
As minds ill bent
Rarely repent,
Untill they meet
Their punishment.

Who more can crave
Then thou hast done:
That gav'st a Sonne,
To free a slave?
First made of nought;
With all since bought.

Sinne, Death, and Hell,
His glorious Name
Quite overcame
Yet I rebell,
And slight the same.

But, I'le come in,
Before my losse,
Me farther tosse,
As sure to win
Under his Crosse.

Ben Jonson

175 *Passiontide Communion*

Not in the Sepulchre Thou art
Till the Third Day shall bid Thee rise;
Thou hast chosen my cold and lifeless heart
To rest as it were Paradise.

Not in the rock-hewn grave Thou'rt laid—
For that were warm beside my chill—
On a hard breast Thou'st leant Thy head
And of cold love Thou hast Thy fill.

Thou had'st Thy Mother's knees, her arm,
And wherefore camest Thou to this strait?
This, that not even Thy love can warm,
A heart deflowered and violate.

But still Thou wilt not rise, be gone,
 Until the Third Day's miracle.
On this impure heart, cold as stone,
 Thou art content and sleepest well.
Katharine Tynan Hinkson

176 *Sonnet LXVIII* from *Amoretti*

Most glorious Lord of lyfe! that, on this day,
Didst make thy triumph over death and sin;
And, having harrowd hell, didst bring away
Captivity thence captive, us to win:
This joyous day, deare Lord, with joy begin;
And grant that we, for whom thou diddest dye,
Being with thy deare blood clene washt from sin,
May live for ever in felicity!
And that thy love we weighing worthily,
May likewise love thee for the same againe;
And for thy sake, that all lyke deare didst buy,
With love may one another entertayne!
 So let us love, deare love, lyke as we ought:
 Love is the lesson which the Lord us taught.
Edmund Spenser

177 *An Easter Canticle*

In every trembling bud and bloom
 That cleaves the earth, a flowery sword,
I see Thee come from out the tomb,
 Thou risen Lord.

In every April wind that sings
 Down lanes that make the heart rejoice;
Yea, in the word the wood-thrush brings,
 I hear Thy voice.

Lo! every tulip is a cup
  To hold Thy morning's brimming wine;
Drink, O my soul, the wonder up—
  Is it not Thine?

The great Lord God, invisible,
  Hath roused to rapture the green grass;
Through sunlit mead and dew-drenched dell,
  I see Him pass.

His old immortal glory wakes
  The rushing streams and emerald hills;
His ancient trumpet softly shakes
  The daffodils.

Thou art not dead! Thou art the whole
  Of life that quickens in the sod;
Green April is Thy very soul,
  Thou great Lord God!

Charles Hanson Towne

178 *Dedication*

When I have ended, then I see
How far my words come short of Thee,
Speech heavenly cannot live on earthly lips,
Pure thoughts borne down to language bear eclipse.

Ah, Christ, what harmony will that be then,
When, in Thy likeness, all the thoughts of men
  Grow satisfied, in silence serving Thee,
  For now, 'tis difference that makes us be
Each clamorous his own meaning to express:
But then all minds will wear the marriage-dress,
  Moving in meet processional degree.

O Christ, come quick, and from the body loose
The long distraction of each present use!
The hands that handle, and the lips that taste
Not at Thy banquet, work but so much waste,
And at sad lingering make heedless haste!

Some day, when love of self hath lost its lust
Of living in me, Thou wilt come, I trust,
And tread my heart to Paradisal dust:
Making me glad, in life's last evening-fall,
To know myself for nought, and Christ for all in all.

Laurence Housman

179 *The Dawning*

Ah! what time wilt Thou come? when shall that cry
"The Bridegroom's coming!" fill the sky?
Shall it in the evening run
When our words and works are done?
Or will Thy all-surprising light
Break at midnight,
When either sleep, or some dark pleasure
Possesseth mad man without measure?
Or shall these early, fragrant hours
Unlock Thy bowers?
And with their blush of light descry
Thy locks crown'd with eternity?

❉

O at what time soever Thou,
Unknown to us, the heavens wilt bow,
And with Thy angels in the van,
Descend to judge poor careless man,
Grant I may not like puddle lie
In a corrupt security,
Where, if a traveller water crave,
He finds it dead, and in a grave;

But at this restless, vocal spring
All day and night doth run and sing,
And though here born, yet is acquainted
Elsewhere, and flowing keeps untainted;
So let me all my busy age
In Thy free services engage;
And though—while here—of course I must
Have commerce sometimes with poor dust,
And in my flesh, though vile and low,
As this doth in her channel flow,
Yet let my course, my aim, my love,
And chief acquaintance be above;
So when that day and hour shall come,
In which Thy Self will be the sun,
Thou'lt find me dress'd and on my way,
Watching the break of Thy great day.

Henry Vaughan

180 *The Way, the Truth, and the Life*

O thou great Friend to all the sons of men,
Who once appeared in humblest guise below,
Sin to rebuke, to break the captive's chain,
To call thy brethren forth from want and woe!

We look to thee; thy truth is still the Light,
Which guides the nations, groping on their way,
Stumbling and falling in disastrous night,
Yet hoping ever for the perfect day.

Yes! Thou art still the Life; thou art the Way
The holiest know;—Light, Life, and Way of heaven!
And they who dearest hope and deepest pray,
Toil by the light, life, way, that thou hast given.

Theodore Parker

IV

THE VARIED MINISTRIES OF NATURE

1 · WITNESS OF FIELD AND FOREST

181 From *Reconciliation*

God of the Granite and the Rose!
  Soul of the Sparrow and the Bee!
The mighty tide of Being flows
  Through countless channels, Lord, from thee.
It leaps to life in grass and flowers,
  Through every grade of being runs,
Till from Creation's radiant towers
  Its glory flames in stars and suns.

❉

God of the Granite and the Rose!
  Soul of the Sparrow and the Bee!
The mighty tide of Being flows
  Through all thy creatures back to Thee.
Thus round and round the circle runs—
  A mighty sea without a shore—
While men and angels, stars and suns,
  Unite to praise Thee evermore!

Elizabeth Doten

182 From *Sincere Praise*

Almighty Maker God!
How wondrous is thy Name!
Thy Glories how diffus'd abroad
Thro' the Creations Frame!

Nature in every Dress
Her humble Homage pays,
And finds a Thousand Ways t'express
Thine undissembled Praise.

In native White and Red
The Rose and Lilly stand,
And free from Pride their Beauties spread
To show thy skilful Hand.

The Lark mounts up the Skie
With unambitious Song,
And bears her Maker's Praise on high
Upon her artless Tongue.

My Soul would rise and sing
To her Creator too,
Fain would my Tongue adore my King
And pay the Worship due.

Isaac Watts

183

Thou Art, O God

Thou art, O God, the life and light
Of all this wondrous world we see;
Its glow by day, its smile by night,
Are but reflections caught from Thee.
Where'er we turn, thy glories shine,
And all things fair and bright are Thine!

❉

When Night, with wings of starry gloom,
O'ershadows all the earth and skies,
Like some dark, beauteous bird, whose plume
Is sparkling with unnumber'd eyes—
That sacred gloom, those fires divine,
So grand, so countless, Lord! are Thine.

When youthful Spring around us breathes,
Thy Spirit warms her fragrant sigh;
And every flower the Summer wreathes
Is born beneath that kindling eye.

Where'er we turn, thy glories shine,
And all things fair and bright are Thine!

Thomas Moore

184 [*Morning Hymn of Adam*] from *Paradise Lost*

These are thy glorious works, parent of good,
Almighty, thine this universal frame,
Thus wondrous fair; thyself how wondrous then!
Unspeakable, who sittest above these heavens
To us invisible or dimly seen
In these thy lowest works, yet these declare
Thy goodness beyond thought, and power divine:
Speak ye who best can tell, ye sons of light,
Angels, for ye behold him, and with songs
And choral symphonies, day without night,
Circle his throne rejoicing, ye in heaven,
On earth join all ye creatures to extol
Him first, him last, him midst, and without end.

❁

Fountains and ye, that warble, as ye flow,
Melodious murmurs, warbling tune his praise.
Join voices all ye living souls, ye birds,
That singing up to heaven gate ascend,
Bear on your wings and in your notes his praise;
Ye that in waters glide, and ye that walk
The earth, and stately tread, or lowly creep;
Witness if I be silent, morn or even,
To hill, or valley, fountain, or fresh shade
Made vocal by my song, and taught his praise.
Hail universal Lord, be bounteous still
To give us only good; and if the night
Have gathered aught of evil or concealed,
Disperse it, as now light dispels the dark.

John Milton

185 *A Chant Out of Doors*

God of grave nights,
God of brave mornings,
God of silent noon,
Hear my salutation!

For where the rapids rage white and scornful,
I have passed safely, filled with wonder;
Where the sweet pools dream under willows,
I have been swimming, filled with life.

God of round hills,
God of green valleys,
God of clean springs,
Hear my salutation!

Where the moose feeds, I have eaten berries,
Where the moose drinks, I have drunk deep.
When the storm crashed through broken heavens—
And under clear skies—I have known joy.

God of great trees,
God of wild grasses,
God of little flowers,
Hear my salutation!

For where the deer crops and the beaver plunges,
Near the river I have pitched my tent;
Where the pines cast aromatic needles
On a still floor, I have known peace.

God of grave nights,
God of brave mornings,
God of silent noon,
Hear my salutation!

Marguerite Wilkinson

186

A Pastoral Hymn

Happy choristers of air,
Who by your nimble flight draw near
  His throne, whose wondrous story
  And unconfined glory
Your notes still carol, whom your sound,
And whom your plumy pipes rebound.

Yet do the lazy snails no less
The greatness of our Lord confess,
  And those whom weight hath chain'd,
  And to the earth restrain'd,
Their ruder voices do as well,
Yea, and the speechless fishes tell.

Great Lord, from whom each tree receives,
Then pays again, as rent, his leaves;
  Thou dost in purple set
  The rose and violet,
And giv'st the sickly lily white;
Yet in them all thy name dost write.

John Hall

187

To God, the Architect

Who thou art I know not,
  But this much I know,
Thou hast set the Pleiades
  In a silver row;

Thou hast sent the trackless winds
  Loose upon their way;
Thou has reared a coloured wall
  'Twixt the night and day;

Thou hast made the flowers to blow,
And the stars to shine,
Hid rare gems and richest ore
In the tunnelled mine—

But chief of all thy wondrous works,
Supreme of all thy plan,
Thou hast put an Upward Reach
In the heart of Man!

Harry Kemp

188

From *A Forest Hymn*

Father, thy hand
Hath reared these venerable columns, thou
Didst weave this verdant roof. Thou didst look down
Upon the naked earth, and, forthwith, rose
All these fair ranks of trees. They, in thy sun,
Budded, and shook their green leaves in thy breeze,
And shot toward heaven. The century-living crow
Whose birth was in their tops, grew old and died
Among their branches, till, at last, they stood,
As now they stand, massy, and tall, and dark,
Fit shrine for humble worshipper to hold
Communion with his Maker.

William Cullen Bryant

189

God, Through All and in You All

God of the earth, the sky, the sea!
Maker of all above, below!
Creation lives and moves in Thee,
Thy present life through all doth flow.

❉

Thy love is in the sunshine's glow,
Thy life is in the quickening air;

When lightnings flash and storm-winds blow,
There is Thy power; Thy law is there.

We feel Thy calm at evening's hour,
Thy grandeur in the march of night;
And, when the morning breaks in power,
We hear Thy word, Let there be light!

But higher far, and far more clear,
Thee in man's spirit we behold;
Thine image and Thyself are there,—
The Indwelling God, proclaimed of old.

Samuel Longfellow

190 *Hymn to the Sun*

Strike down into my breast, O sun, and cleanse my soul—
Shadows are here and ailments of the dark!
Burn out the horror, sear away the dread,
Beat like live hope in spark on molten spark.

Lone in your uncouth solitude of chasmed air
You scale the sky, reckless of end or change,
Chanting like some wild Himalayan shepherd
Wind-rocked, enraptured, on his bleak vast range.

Eternity will pass and down the blue cliffs hear
You singing, vigorous still in fierce delight.
Strike through my breast and pour your courage in—
Enough to last this little way to night.

William Alexander Percy

191 *Out-of-Doors*

God, what a day it is to be abroad!
To walk as one were winged, snatch at the breeze,
Stand up against the stature of the trees,

Feel freedom stretching on, an endless road;
To lift arms high akimbo, laugh and run,
And challenge all the spaces of the sun.
Robert Whitaker

192 *Wind in the Pine*

Oh, I can hear you, God, above the cry
Of the tossing trees—
Rolling your windy tides across the sky,
And splashing your silver seas
Over the pine,
To the water-line
Of the moon.
Oh, I can hear you, God,
Above the wail of the lonely loon—
When the pine-tops pitch and nod—
Chanting your melodies
Of ghostly waterfalls and avalanches,
Washing your wind among the branches
To make them pure and white.

Wash over me, God, with your piney breeze
And your moon's wet-silver pool;
Wash over me, God, with your wind and night,
And leave me clean and cool.
Lew Sarett

193 *A Prayer*

O Earth, O dewy mother, breathe on us
Something of all thy beauty and thy might,
Us that are part of day, but most of night,
Not strong like thee, but ever burdened thus
With glooms and cares, things pale and dolorous
Whose gladdest moments are not wholly bright;
Something of all thy freshness and thy light,

O Earth, O mighty mother, breathe on us.
O mother, who wast long before our day,
And after us full many an age shalt be,
Careworn and blind, we wander from thy way:
Born of thy strength, yet weak and halt are we;
Grant us, O mother, therefore, us who pray,
Some little of thy light and majesty.

Archibald Lampman

194

A Sailor's Prayer

Lord, Lord to Thee
Who stilled the waves
That day on Galilee—
We give our thanks
That Thou hast made
The turmoil of the sea. . . .

All green and white
From cutting prow
Is dashed the flying spray,
As 'round about
In chorus roar
The billows as the play;
Though groan the ribs
With every blow. . . .
Though reeling are the skies. . . .
What mariner,
Lord of us all,
Would have it otherwise?

Let overhead
The creaking yards
Shout warnings to the sails
Whose canvas breasts
Expand with fierce
Resistance to the gales;

Let underfoot
Be decks awash
With sheets of racing foam....
For, Master, then
And only then
Are sailormen
At home!

Lord, Lord to Thee
Who taught us Faith
That day on Galilee,
We give our thanks
That Thou hast made—
The turmoil of the sea!

George Hornell Morris

195 *The Comparison and Complaint*

Infinite Power, eternal Lord,
  How sovereign is thy hand!
All nature rose to obey thy word,
  And moves at thy command.

With steady course thy shining sun
  Keeps his appointed way;
And all the hours obedient run
  The circle of the day.

But ah! how wide my spirit flies,
  And wanders from her God!
My soul forgets the heavenly prize,
  And treads the downward road.

The raging fire, and stormy sea,
  Perform thine awful will,
And every beast and every tree,
  Thy great designs fulfil:

While my wild passions rage within,
  Nor thy commands obey;
And flesh and sense, enslav'd to sin,
  Draw my best thoughts away.

Shall creatures of a meaner frame
  Pay all thy dues to thee;
Creatures, that never knew thy name,
  That never lov'd like me?

Great God, create my soul anew,
  Conform my heart to thine,
Melt down my will and let it flow,
  And take the mould divine.

Seize my whole frame into thy hand;
  Here all my powers I bring;
Manage the wheels by thy command,
  And govern every spring.

Then shall my feet no more depart,
  Nor wandering senses rove;
Devotion shall be all my heart,
  And all my passions love.

Then not the sun shall more than I
  His Maker's law perform,
Nor travel swifter through the sky,
  Nor with a zeal so warm.

Isaac Watts

196

Sonnet

On hearing the *Dies Irae* Sung in the Sistine Chapel.

Nay, Lord, not thus! white lilies in the spring,
  Sad olive-groves, or silver-breasted dove,

  Teach me more clearly of Thy life and love
Than terrors of red flame and thundering.
The hillside vines dear memories of Thee bring:
  A bird at evening flying to its nest
  Tells me of One who had no place of rest:
I think it is of Thee the sparrows sing.
Come rather on some autumn afternoon,
  When red and brown are burnished on the leaves,
  And the fields echo to the gleaner's song,
Come when the splendid fulness of the moon
  Looks down upon the rows of golden sheaves,
  And reap Thy harvest: we have waited long.

Oscar Wilde

2 · LORD, MAKE US AWARE

197 From *Thanks from Earth to Heaven*

Holy Poet, I have heard
Thy lost music, Thy least word;
Not Thy beauty's tiniest part
Has escaped this loving heart!

While the great world goes its way
I watch in wonder all the day,
All the night my spirit sings
For the loveliness of things.

John Hall Wheelock

198 *Lord of the Far Horizons*

Lord of the far horizons,
Give us the eyes to see
Over the verge of sundown
The beauty that is to be.
Give us the skill to fashion
The task of thy command,
Eager to follow the pattern
We may not understand.

Masters of ancient wisdom
And the lore lost long ago,
Inspire our foolish reason
With faith to seek and know.
When the skein of truth is tangled
And the lead of sense is blind,
Foster the fire to lighten
Our unillumined mind.

Lord of the lilac ranges
That lift on the flawless blue,
Grant us the heart of rapture
The earlier ages knew—
The spirit glad and ungrudging,
And light as the mountain air,
To walk with the Sons of Morning
Through the glory of Earth the fair.

Bliss Carman

199 *Common Blessings*

Lord of my years, can life be bare
With beauty springing everywhere?

Can I forlorn and lonely be
With sweet bird-song from every tree?

Can I succumb to doubt and fear
With tasks to do and friends to cheer?

What matters it that I am poor
With roses blooming at my door?
My garden is a maze of gold
As summer hours their dreams unfold.

Can I complain, by sorrows pent,
Knowing I have the boon, content?

Trouble shall flee and fear take wing,
For life still brings me songs to sing....

Lord of my days, how thankful I
For a thankful heart, as life goes by!

Thomas Curtis Clark

200 *Prayer*

Lord, make me sensitive to the sight
Of swallows in their graceful flight;
Let each dip, each swoop, each glide
Forever in my heart abide.

A darkened steeple against the sky,
A firefly's gleam where shadows lie,
Lightning that splits the sky apart—
Let each of thy miracles pierce my heart!

Then, though blindness be my curse,
The wonders of this universe
Will be so mirrored in my soul,
I'll not need eyes to make me whole.

Barbara Marr

201 *A Page's Road Song*

(13th Century)

Jesu,
If Thou wilt make
Thy peach trees bloom for me,
And fringe my bridle path both sides
With tulips, red and free,
If Thou wilt make Thy skies as blue
As ours in Sicily,
And wake the little leaves that sleep
On every bending tree—
I promise not to vexen Thee
That Thou shouldst make eternally
Heaven my home;
But right contentedly,
A singing page I'll be
Here, in Thy springtime,
Jesu.

William Alexander Percy

202 O Love, That Dost with Goodness Crown

O Love, that dost with goodness crown
The years through all the ages down,
Our highest faith, our deepest cheer,
Is that thy life is ever near!

From planets singing on their way
To flowers that fear the eye of day,
From rivers that rejoicing go
To brooks that murmur sweet and low,

Well know I that the pageant vast,
So beautiful from first to last,
Is but the smile upon thy face,
The sign of love's unmeasured grace.

The seasons roll at thy command;
'Tis in thy strength the mountains stand;
And rooted are all things that bless
Deep in thy everlastingness.

Within thy circling arms we lie,
Safe-lapped in thine infinity,
O Love, who dost with goodness crown
The moments and the ages down!

John W. Chadwick

203 A Prayer

Each day I walk with wonder
'Neath skies or dark or fair;
Over, around, and under
Are marvels that I share.

Whate'er the bonds of duty,
The gyves that grip and thrall,

The luring call of beauty
Is greater than them all.

I pray I may be shriven
Should I fail more or less,—
That I may be forgiven
For following loveliness!
Clinton Scollard

204 From *Impiety*

Lord, I have not time to pray
Before the asters blow,
And should I enter in Thy church
Perchance I miss the glow
Of branches bright with glint of snow.

Ah Lord, Thou shouldst not ask of me
One hour spent in prayer,
For fear some quiet rain let fall
Its shining hair,
And I, who longed for rain, might not be there.

I do not want, my Lord, to give
One breath of life to Thee.
I have so little time to live;
Thou hast eternity.
Helene Margaret

205 *If I Have Lifted Up Mine Eyes to Admire*

If I have lifted up mine eyes to admire
The moon that walks in brightness on the hills,
Or kissed my hand to see the milky fire
That over sea and over land she spills;
If I have suffered my rash thought to range

About the greater light that rules the day
In impious scrutiny, or let like strange
Imaginations in my heart hold sway;
If I have been complacent to arrest
My gaze upon these things that do appear:
This bloom of flesh in which the soul is dressed,
Or said of art, "Behold what stones are here!"
O Thou who in Thy wisdom made all these,
Forgive the mortal's fond idolatries.

Amos N. Wilder

206 *Let Me Flower as I Will*

God, let me flower as I will!
For I am weary of the chill
Companionship of cloistered vines
And hothouse-nurtured columbines;
Oh, weary of the pruning-knife
That shapes my prim decorous life—
Of clambering trellises that hold me,
Of flawless patterned forms that mold me.

God, let me flower as I will!
A shaggy rambler on the hill—
Familiar with April's growing pain
Of green buds bursting after rain.
Oh, let me hear among the sheaves
Of autumn, the song of wistful leaves,
The lullaby of the brook that dallies
Among the high blue mountain valleys.
And may my comrades be but these:
Birds on the bough, and guzzling bees
Among my blossoms, as they sup
On the dew in my silver-petaled cup.

God, let my parching roots go deep
Among the cold green springs, and keep

Firm grip upon the mossy edges
Of imperishable granite ledges,
That thus my body may withstand
The avalanche of snow and sand,
The trample of the years, the flail
Of whipping wind and bouncing hail.
And when December with its shroud
Of fallen snow and leaden cloud,
Shall find me in the holiday
Of slumber, shivering and gray
Against the sky—and in the end,
My somber days shall hold no friend
But a whimpering wolf, and on the tree
A frozen bird—so may it be.
For in that day I shall have won
The glory of the summer sun;
My leaves, by windy fingers played,
An eerie music shall have made;
I shall have known in some far land
The tender comfort of a Hand
And the liquid beauty of a Tongue
That finds its syllables among
Wild wind and waterfall and rill—
God, let me flower as I will!

Lew Sarett

207 *A Prayer*

Teach me, Father, how to go
Softly as the grasses grow;
Hush my soul to meet the shock
Of the wild world as a rock;
But my spirit, propt with power,
Make as simple as a flower.
Let the dry heart fill its cup,
Like a poppy looking up;
Let life lightly wear her crown,

Like a poppy looking down,
When its heart is filled with dew,
And its life begins anew.

Teach me, Father, how to be
Kind and patient as a tree.
Joyfully the crickets croon
Under shady oak at noon;
Beetle, on his mission bent,
Tarries in that cooling tent.
Let me, also, cheer a spot,
Hidden field or garden grot—
Place where passing souls can rest
On the way and be their best.

Edwin Markham

208 *Judge Not According to the Appearance*

Lord, purge our eyes to see
Within the seed a tree,
  Within the glowing egg a bird,
    Within the shroud a butterfly:

Till taught by such, we see
Beyond all creatures Thee,
  And hearken for Thy tender word,
    And hear it, "Fear not: it is I."

Christina G. Rossetti

209 *O Thou Eternal Source of Life*

O Thou Eternal Source of Life,
  Of all that breathes, a part,
Amid the world's unceasing strife,
  Grant us the seeing heart.

Help us to see in all that lives
The same immortal fire
Which makes its home in man, and gives
Him hope and new desire.

Grant us who breathe and are akin
To creatures, great and small,
A life-revering heart within,
That bows before them all.

Remove from us the love to kill,
That slays with cruel hand;
Grant us the joy that works no ill,
But seeks to understand.

Yet grant us, Lord, the seeing eye
That calls not all things one,
But feels the death that all must die
As fuller life is won.

Rolland W. Schloerb

210

Prayer for the Useless Days

Do not leave me, Lord, do not let the field lie fallow
Year after year, hour after sullen hour,
Till the clay grows hard and the lonely land grows sour
Under a winter sky one-toned and sallow.

There are varying griefs, there are many kinds of trouble:
Thistles and thorns can spawn and choke the seed,
But a world tramped down by time is worse than weed.
Not a mixture of wheat and tare but a rotting stubble.

Come husbandman, come Lord, and crack the clod!
Come with a fork and plow, come with a harrow.
Fling to the open winds the funeral barrow.
Do not leave me, God.

Edith Lovejoy Pierce

3 · PRAYERS IN SEASON

211 *A Prayer in Spring*

Oh, give us pleasure in the flowers to-day;
And give us not to think so far away
As the uncertain harvest; keep us here
All simply in the springing of the year.

Oh, give us pleasure in the orchard white,
Like nothing else by day, like ghosts by night;
And make us happy in the happy bees,
The swarm dilating round the perfect trees.

And make us happy in the darting bird
That suddenly above the bees is heard,
The meteor that thrusts in with needle bill,
And off a blossom in mid air stands still.

For this is love and nothing else is love,
The which it is reserved for God above
To sanctify to what far ends He will,
But which it only needs that we fulfil.

Robert Frost

212 From *A Little Te Deum of the Commonplace*

With hearts responsive
And enfranchised eyes,
We thank Thee, Lord,—

For those first tiny, prayerful-folded hands
That pierce the winter's crust, and softly bring
Life out of death, the endless mystery;—

For all the first sweet flushings of the Spring;
The greening earth, the tender heavenly blue;
The rich brown furrows gaping for the seed;
For all Thy grace in bursting bud and leaf,—
The bridal sweetness of the orchard trees,
Rose-tender in their coming fruitfulness;
The fragrant snow-drifts flung upon the breeze;
The grace and glory of the fruitless flowers,
Ambrosial beauty their reward and ours;
For hedgerows sweet with hawthorn and wild rose;
For meadows spread with gold and gemmed with stars;
For every tint of every tiniest flower;
For every daisy smiling to the sun;
For every bird that builds in joyous hope;
For every lamb that frisks beside its dam;
For every leaf that rustles in the wind;
For spiring poplar, and for spreading oak;
For queenly birch, and lofty swaying elm;
For the great cedar's benedictory grace;
For earth's ten thousand fragrant incenses,—
Sweet altar-gifts from leaf and fruit and flower;
For every wondrous thing that greens and grows;
For the wide-spread cornlands,—billowing golden seas;
For rippling stream, and white-laced waterfall;
For purpling mountains; lakes like silver shields;
For white-piled clouds that float against the blue;
For tender green of far-off upland slopes;
For fringing forests and far-gleaming spires;
For those white peaks, serene and grand and still;
For that deep sea—a shallow to Thy love;
For round green hills, earth's full benignant breasts;
For sun-chased shadows flitting o'er the plain;
For gleam and gloom; for all life's counter-change;
For hope that quickens under darkening skies;
For all we see; for all that underlies,—
We thank Thee, Lord!

John Oxenham

213 *Prayer in April*

God grant that I may never be
A scoffer at Eternity—
As long as every April brings
The sweet rebirth of growing things;
As long as grass is green anew,
As long as April's skies are blue,
I shall believe that God looks down
Upon His wide earth, cold and brown,
To bless its unborn mystery
Of leaf, and bud, and flower to be;
To smile on it from tender skies—
How could I think it otherwise?
Had I been dust for many a year,
I still would know when Spring was near,
For the good earth that pillowed me
Would whisper immortality,
And I, in part, would rise and sing
Amid the grasses murmuring.
When looking on the mother sod,
Can I hold doubt that this be God?
Or when a primrose smiles at me,
Can I distrust Eternity?

Sara Henderson Hay

214 *A Prayer*

Tend me my birds, and bring again
The brotherhood of woodland life,
So shall I wear the seasons round,
A friend to need, a foe to strife.

Keep me my heritage of lawn,
And grant me, Father, till I die
The fine sincerity of light
And luxury of open sky.

So, learning always, may I find
  My heaven around me everywhere,
And go in hope from this to Thee,
  The pupil of Thy country air.

Norman Gale

215 *Why, Lord*

Why, Lord, must something in us
  Yearly die?
And our most true remembrance of it
  Lie?
Until the pure forgetting
  By and by.

Why then must something other
  Come and grow?
Renewing us for nothing, save the
  Slow
Upbuilding of this bed
  Of needles, so.

Why is the soil not bitter
  Where we stand?
Whose, Lord, upon our roots
  The sweetening hand?
For so it is: we love
  No shallower land.

Mark Van Doren

216 *Prayer for This Day*

Here, west of winter, lies the ample flower
Along a bough not builded on by snow.
Now earth conceives the bridal and the bower;
Now what was rain is vistas in a row
Of spring, or miles of water knocking upon stone.

The random green heals over without flaw,
Hills heave a bright front to the midmast sun.
Oh, what are we to say that worlds are lost,
Or what bears heaviest on the heart almost?

Still to a century superb for death
The emerald shrub again, the rose undwindled.
Still quail are whistling with a bubble's breath
And lean and tender lilies taper still;
Still satin moths at night with great eyes kindled
Throb into flame. It is no time to will
Prayer from a heart too long by reason fondled,
But here where flinty branches loosen into white,
Here at the balmy side of spring's rebirth
Kneel down. We ask no vision, no heavenly light,
But the patience and poise of flowers from the earth.

Hildegarde Flanner

217

Touring

God of Summer—I have seen
World on world of summer green—
Summer earth and summer sky,
Fields of summer turning by;
Hills beyond us fall away,
Tumbled slopes in disarray,
Fold and melt into a plain:
Fire and gold of summer grain.

Orchards curving on a hill,
Heavy-fruited, green and still,
Heave a shoulder to the sky,
Bend and bow and hurry by;
Fields of clover burn and pass,
Cattle knee-deep in the grass
Lift a lazy head and look
Pictures in a picture-book. . . .

Corn in swift, revolving rows,
Dripping sunlight where it goes,
Wheels and glitters and returns:
Bladed beauty's lifted urns;
Woods all shadowed, cooling earth,
Murmuring of a quiet mirth,
Pour damp odours where they pass,
Breath of fern and earth and grass. . . .
Ramblers on a lichened wall,
Ramblers, ramblers pouring all
Colour that the world has known
Out upon an aging stone.—
Little towns of street and spire,
Dooryard roses, heart's desire,
Light a dream within the mind,
Light a dream . . . and fall behind.

God of mercies—when I slept,
World on world of summer kept
Turning, turning softly by,—
Summer earth and summer sky:
Fields of summer that will be
Summer always unto me—
Never lost, not left behind:
Always summer for my mind.

David Morton

218 *Grace for Gardens*

Lord God in Paradise,
  Look upon our sowing,
Bless the little gardens
  And good green growing!
Give us sun,
  Give us rain,
Bless the orchards
  And the grain!

Lord God in Paradise,
  Please bless the beans and peas,
Give us full corn on the ear,
  We will praise you, Lord, for these.
Bless the blossom,
  And the fruit.
Bless the seed
  And the root!

Lord God in Paradise,
  Over my brown field is seen,
Trembling and adventuring,
  A miracle of green.
Send such grace
  As you know
To keep it safe
  And make it grow!

Lord God in Paradise,
  For the wonder of the seed
Wondering, we thank you, while
  We tell you of our need.

Look down from Paradise,
  Look upon our sowing.
Bless the little gardens
  And good green growing.
Give us sun,
  Give us rain,
Bless the orchards
  And the grain!

Louise Driscoll

V

BY DAY AND NIGHT

219 *Come, O Lord, Like Morning Sunlight*

Come, O Lord, like morning sunlight,
Making all life new and free;
For the daily task and challenge
May we rise renewed in Thee.

Come, O Lord, like ocean flood-tides
Flowing inland from the sea;
As the waters fill the shallows,
May our souls be filled with Thee.

Come, O Lord, like mountain breezes,
Freshening life in vale and lea;
In the heat and stress of duty
May our souls find strength in Thee.

Come, O Lord, like evening twilight,
Bringing peace on land and sea;
At the radiant close of labor
May our souls find rest in Thee.

Milton S. Littlefield

220 *Vespers*

Twilight falls on the hill.
The west is a crumble of sundown.
From hollow and cavern and cranny
The shadows lengthen and creep.
And a slow singing of far bells
Blows on the breath of the evening
From the dim-piled crepuscular mountains
And intricate valleys of sleep.

Lamp after lamp shines forth
From the scattered farm windows below me.
A lantern moves by the rick.
Cattle low at the bars.
Comes the dull rumble of barn doors.
Voices of weary children
Dwindle into the dusk. . .
Night—and the stars!

God, if thou grantest me Heaven,
Take not this beauty from me,
But down from the lonely sky
Send thou my spirit again,
Back to the old worn ways
Of this little flickering planet—
Back to the grief and the toil
And the hopes and the homes of men.

Odell Shepard

221 *Saviour, Whose Love Is Like the Sun*

Saviour, whose love is like the sun,
  But knows no western track of night,
Shine on our souls when day is done,
  That eventide may still be light.

Thine was the light that cheered our way
  Through youth's desire and manhood's deed;
Now at the ending of the day
  Peace at the last is all our need.

Give Thou that peace, O Saviour dear!
  For Thou hast overcome with might
Death, and our sins, and every fear,
  And opened heaven for our delight.

Howard Chandler Robbins

222 From *Evening*

Abide with us: for it is toward evening,
and the day is far spent. Luke 24:29

'Tis gone, that bright and orbed blaze,
Fast fading from our wistful gaze;
Yon mantling cloud has hid from sight
The last faint pulse of quivering light.

In darkness and in weariness
The traveller on his way must press,
No gleam to watch on tree or tower,
Whiling away the lonesome hour.

Sun of my soul! Thou Saviour dear,
It is not night if Thou be near:
Oh may no earth-born cloud arise
To hide thee from thy servant's eyes.

When round the wondrous works below
My searching rapturous glance I throw,
Tracing out Wisdom, Power and Love,
In earth and sky, in stream or grove;—

Or by the light thy words disclose
Watch Time's full river as it flows,
Scanning thy gracious Providence,
Where not too deep for mortal sense:—

When with dear friends sweet talk I hold,
And all the flowers of life unfold;—
Let not my heart within me burn,
Except in all I Thee discern.

When the soft dews of kindly sleep
My wearied eyelids gently steep,

Be my last thought, how sweet to rest
For ever on my Saviour's breast.

Abide with me from morn till eve,
For without Thee I cannot live:
Abide with me when night is nigh,
For without Thee I dare not die.

❊

Come near and bless us when we wake,
Ere through the world our way we take:
Till in the ocean of thy love
We lose ourselves in heaven above.

John Keble

223 *Prayer by Moonlight*

No leaf is left unmoistened by the dew
Tonight, no single blade unglittering
With the moon's mica fallen to the grass.
How swift your hours until the moon must pass
To sun once more, and dry leaves in the tree,
And the bells that sound from Holy Trinity,
And children summer crisp along the path!
Only the tower there will be as tense;
Only the table of the truth as still.

Feed me no wafer but experience!
No wine but the rich garnet pour of time
Tasting of pain and danger as you will.

Roberta Teale Swartz

224 *Evensong*[1]

The embers of the day are red
Beyond the murky hill.
The kitchen smokes: the bed

[1] Written at Vailma.

In the darkling house is spread:
The great sky darkens overhead,
And the great woods are shrill.
So far have I been led,
Lord, by Thy will:
So far I have followed, Lord, and wondered still.

The breeze from the embalmèd land
Blows sudden toward the shore,
And claps my cottage door.
I hear the signal, Lord—I understand.
The night at Thy command
Comes. I will eat and sleep and will not question more.

Robert Louis Stevenson

225 *Grace Before Sleep*

How can our minds and bodies be
Grateful enough that we have spent
Here in this generous room, we three,
This evening of content?
Each one of us has walked through storm
And fled the wolves along the road;
But here the hearth is wide and warm,
And for this shelter and this light
Accept, O Lord, our thanks to-night.

Sara Teasdale

226 *A Child's Evening Prayer*

Ere on my bed my limbs I lay,
God grant me grace my prayers to say:
O God! preserve my mother dear
In strength and health for many a year;

And, O! preserve my father too,
And may I pay him reverence due;
And may I my best thoughts employ
To be my parents' hope and joy;
And, O! preserve my brothers both
From evil doings and from sloth,
And may we always love each other,
Our friends, our father, and our mother,
And still, O Lord, to me impart
An innocent and grateful heart,
That after my last sleep I may
Awake to thy eternal day!

Samuel T. Coleridge

227 *The Light of Stars*

Slowly, by God's hand unfurled,
Down around the weary world
Falls the darkness; O how still
Is the working of His will!

Mighty Spirit, here am I!
Work in me as silently;
Veil the day's distracting sights,
Show me heaven's eternal lights.

Living worlds to view be brought
In the boundless realms of thought;
High and infinite desires,
Flaming like those upper fires.

Holy Truth, eternal Right,
Let them break upon the sight;
Let them shine serene and still,
And with light my being fill.

William H. Furness

228 From *Evening Hymn*

O God, whose daylight leadeth down
Into the sunless way,
Who with restoring sleep dost crown
The labor of the day!

What I have done, Lord, make it clean
With thy forgiveness dear;
That so to-day what might have been,
To-morrow may appear.

George Macdonald

229 *A Prayer for Peace*

Father in Heaven! humbly before thee
Kneeling in prayer thy children appear;
We in our weakness, we in our blindness,
Thou in thy wisdom, hear us, oh hear!

God watching o'er us sleeps not nor slumbers,
Faithful night watches his angels keep.
Through all the darkness, unto the dawning,
To his beloved he giveth sleep.

Edward Rowland Sill

230 *Communion*

Lord, I have knelt and tried to pray to-night,
But thy love came upon me like a sleep,
And all desire died out; upon the deep
Of thy mere love I lay, each thought in light
Dissolving like the sunset clouds, at rest
Each tremulous wish, and my strength weakness, sweet
As a sick boy with soon o'erwearied feet

Finds, yielding him unto his mother's breast
To weep for weakness there. I could not pray,
But with closed eyes I felt thy bosom's love
Beating toward mine, and then I would not move
Till of itself the joy should pass away;
At last my heart found voice,—"Take me, O Lord,
And do with me according to thy word."

Edward Dowden

231 *Insomnia*

E'en this, Lord, didst thou bless—
This pain of sleeplessness—
  The livelong night,
Urging God's gentlest angel from thy side,
That anguish only might with thee abide
  Until the light.
Yea, e'en the last and best,
Thy victory and rest,
  Came thus to thee;
For 'twas while others calmly slept around,
That thou alone in sleeplessness wast found
  To comfort me.

John Banister Tabb

232 *Lux in Tenebris*

At night what things will stalk abroad,
  What veilèd shapes, and eyes of dread!
With phantoms in a lonely road
  And visions of the dead.

The kindly room when day is here,
  At night takes ghostly terrors on;
And every shadow hath its fear,
  And every wind its moan.

Lord Jesus, Day-star of the world,
  Rise Thou, and bid this dark depart,
And all the east, a rose uncurled,
  Grow golden at the heart!

Lord, in the watches of the night,
  Keep Thou my soul! a trembling thing
As any moth that in daylight
  Will spread a rainbow wing.

Katharine Tynan Hinkson

233 *Strange, All-Absorbing Love*

Strange, all-absorbing Love, who gatherest
Unto Thy glowing all my pleasant dew,
Then delicately my garden waterest,
Drawing the old, to pour it back anew:

In the dim glitter of the dawning hours
"Not so," I said, "but still these drops of light,
Heart-shrined among the petals of my flowers,
Shall hold the memory of the starry night

"So fresh, no need of showers shall there be."—
Ah, senseless gardener! must it come to pass
That 'neath the glaring noon thou shouldst see
Thine earth become as iron, His heavens as brass?

Nay rather, O my Sun, I will be wise,
Believe in Love which may not yet be seen,
Yield Thee my earth-drops, call Thee from the skies,
In soft return, to keep my bedding green.

So when the bells at Vesper-tide shall sound,
And the dead ocean o'er my garden flows,
Upon the Golden Altar may be found
Some scarlet berries and a Christmas rose.

Digby Mackworth Dolben

234

Prayer at Dawn

Now we begin another day together.
The night has clutched the darkness to her breast
And vanished slowly westward. Gaily dressed
In brightly burnished brass and polished leather,
The East's great army comes. No matter whether
It brings us sun, and songs of love to sing,
Or cloud and terror; we shall slip its tether
And walk today for joy of journeying.
If I must weep, thy rain my tears' delight,
If I may laugh, thy wind my laughter's flight;
Thy wealth to compensate the day's default,
Thy power to fend the ultimate assault.
Let life be grave as pain or light as feather,
Now we begin another day together.

Edwin McNeill Poteat

235

Mattens

I cannot ope mine eyes,
But thou art ready there to catch
My morning-soul and sacrifice:
Then we must needs for that day make a match.

My God, what is a heart?
Silver, or gold, or precious stone,
Or starre, or rainbow, or a part
Of all these things, or all of them in one?

My God, what is a heart,
That thou shouldst it so eye, and wooe,
Powring upon it all thy art,
As if that thou hadst nothing els to do?

Indeed mans whole estate
Amounts (and richly) to serve thee:

He did not heav'n and earth create,
Yet studies them, not him by whom they be.

Teach me thy love to know;
That this new light, which now I see,
May both the work and workman show:
Then by a sunne-beam I will climbe to thee.

George Herbert

236 *Sung on a Sunny Morning*

Oh, holy cause
That points the grass
And lifts the flower,
That gives to rain
And slanting grain
And sun just dower,
Confirm your laws!
Ever flood
My sweetened blood
With lenient power;
Keep me free
Eternally
As in this hour.

Jean Starr Untermeyer

237 *Not to be Ministered To*

O Lord, I pray
That for this day
I may not swerve
By foot or hand
From Thy command,
Not to be served, but to serve.

This, too, I pray,
That for this day

No love of ease
Nor pride prevent
My good intent,
Not to be pleased, but to please.

And if I may,
I'd have this day
Strength from above
To set my heart
In heavenly art,
Not to be loved, but to love.

Maltbie D. Babcock

238

Prayer for Dreadful Morning

Long have I loved the terrible clouds that loom
Like galleons of the Armada of the air
Whose carronades flame golden in the gloom,
Shattering houses like some wild corsair.
And I have loved the baying suns that chase
Night, the grey wolf, before their gorgeous pack
In view-halloo across the void of space—
The golden wolf-hounds of the zodiac.
Better the thunder's tocsin, and the torch
Of lightning, and the tempest's *Carmagnole*—
Better the hounds of flame whose great jaws scorch
Earth's tawny outer soil, Man's inner soul—
Bursting in Dreadful Morning on our gloom,
Than that the world should stay a stuffy room!

E. Merrill Root

VI

THE HOME CIRCLE

239 *Wedding-Hymn*

Thou God, whose high, eternal Love
Is the only blue sky of our life,
Clear all the Heaven that bends above
The life-road of this man and wife.

May these two lives be but one note
In the world's strange-sounding harmony,
Whose sacred music e'er shall float
Through every discord up to Thee.

As when from separate stars two beams
Unite to form one tender ray:
As when two sweet but shadowy dreams
Explain each other in the day:

So may these two dear hearts one light
Emit, and each interpret each.
Let an angel come and dwell to-night
In this dear double-heart, and teach!

Sidney Lanier

240 *The Sanctum*

Lord, God of love, the wedded hearts'
Sure Comforter,
O! make mine pure in all its parts,
For Thee and Her!
Pour, Lord, the flood-tide of Thy grace
Through all its chambers, and efface
Each secret thought's abiding place.
I pray Thee make
One shrine of it, which Thou and she

May jointly share, that it may be
Open to her, Lord, as to Thee,
  For her dear sake.

Lord, God of love, who givest me
  Her heart of fire,
Long keep it mine, but let it be
  Not mine entire.
Though mine the honeyed tenderness,
That wells therein to cheer and bless
When joys elate or cares depress,
  I pray Thee make
Thy secret shrine within its core.
Let me before one close-sealed door
Cry "Non sum dignus" o'er and o'er
  For her dear sake.

Thomas Augustus Daly

241

A Prayer for a Marriage

We have shared beauty and have shared grief, too;
And these have brought us nearer than we knew.
We have shared joy and loneliness and fear,
Danger and terror and death creeping near
Joined us. The worst that poverty can do
Will not avail, though all its strength is bent
Against us. Naught on earth can part us two,
Save the monotony of calm content.

Pray God that He may give a little pain,
A fear, a joy, to draw us close again.
Where'er our pleasant paths too smoothly run,
May storm-clouds change the gold of too much sun.

Mary Carolyn Davies

242

Prayer for a New House

May nothing evil cross this door,
And may ill-fortune never pry

About these windows; may the roar
  And rains go by.

Strengthened by faith, these rafters will
  Withstand the battering of the storm;
This hearth, tho all the world grow chill,
  Will keep us warm.

Peace shall walk softly through these rooms,
  Touching our lips with holy wine,
Till every casual corner blooms
  Into a shrine.

Laughter shall drown the raucous shout;
  And, tho these sheltering walls are thin,
May they be strong to keep hate out
  And hold love in.

Louis Untermeyer

243 *O Thou Whose Gracious Presence Blest*

O Thou whose gracious presence blest
  The home at Bethany,
This shelter from the world's unrest,
This home made ready for its Guest,
  We dedicate to Thee.

When Thou didst pass the Temple gate,
  To pray beneath its dome,
It was Thy Father's House, more great
Because by love made consecrate;
  It was Thine only home.

We build an altar here, and pray
  That Thou wilt show Thy face.
Dear Lord, if Thou wilt come to stay,

This home we consecrate to-day
  Will be a Holy Place.

Louis F. Benson

244 *House Blessing*

Bless the four corners of this house,
  And be the lintel blest;
And bless the hearth and bless the board
  And bless each place of rest;
And bless the door that opens wide
  To stranger as to kin;
And bless each crystal window-pane
  That lets the starlight in;
And bless the rooftree overhead
  And every sturdy wall.
The peace of man, the peace of God,
  The peace of Love on all!

Arthur Guiterman

245 *O Blessèd House, That Cheerfully Receiveth*

O blessèd house, that cheerfully receiveth
  Thy visits, Jesus Christ, the soul's true Friend,
That, far beyond all other guests, believeth
  It must to Thee its warmest cheer extend;
Where ev'ry heart to Thee is fondly turning,
  Where ev'ry eye for Thee with pleasure speaks,
Where all to know Thy will are truly yearning,
  And ev'ry one to do it promptly seeks.

O blessèd house, where man and wife, united
  In Thy true love, have both one heart and mind,
Where both to Thy salvation are invited,
  And in Thy doctrine both contentment find;
Where both, to Thee, in truth, for ever cleaving

In joy, in grief, make Thee their only stay,
And fondly hope in Thee to be believing,
Both in the good and in the evil day.

O blessèd house, where little children tender
Are laid upon Thy heart, with hands of prayer,
Thou Friend of children, Who wilt freely render
To them more than a mother's loving care,
Where round Thy feet they gather, to Thee clinging,
And hear Thy loving voice most willingly,
And in their songs, Thy hearty praises ringing,
Rejoice in Thee, O blessèd Lord, in Thee.

Karl Johann Philipp Spitta
Tr. Charles William Schaeffer

246 *A Thanksgiving to God, for His House*

Lord, Thou hast given me a cell
Wherein to dwell;
And little house, whose humble Roof
Is weather-proof;
Under the sparres of which I lie
Both soft, and drie;
Where Thou my chamber for to ward
Hast set a Guard
Of harmlesse thoughts, to watch and keep
Me, while I sleep.
Low is my porch, as is my Fate,
Both void of state;
And yet the threshold of my doore
Is worn by'th poore,
Who thither come, and freely get
Good words, or meat:
Like as my Parlour, so my Hall
And Kitchin's small:
A little Butterie, and therein
A little Byn,

Which keeps my little loafe of Bread
 Unchipt, unflead:
Some brittle sticks of Thorne or Briar
 Make me a fire,
Close by whose living coale I sit,
 And glow like it.
Lord, I confesse too, when I dine,
 The Pulse is Thine,
And all those other Bits, that bee
 There plac'd by Thee;
The Worts, the Purslain, and the Messe
 Of Water-cresse,
Which of Thy kindnesse Thou hast sent;
 And my content
Makes those, and my beloved Beet,
 To be more sweet.
'Tis Thou that crown'st my glittering Hearth
 With guiltlesse mirth;
And giv'st me Wassaile Bowles to drink,
 Spic'd to the brink.
Lord, 'tis Thy plenty-dropping hand,
 That soiles my land;
And giv'st me, for my Bushell sowne,
 Twice ten for one:
Thou mak'st my teeming Hen to lay
 Her egg each day:
Besides my healthfull Ewes to beare
 Me twins each yeare:
The while the conduits of my Kine
 Run Creame, (for Wine.)
All these, and better Thou dost send
 Me, to this end,
That I should render, for my part,
 A thankfull heart;
Which, fir'd with incense, I resigne,
 As wholly Thine;

But the acceptance, that must be,
My Christ, by Thee.

Robert Herrick

247 *At a Window*

Give me hunger,
O you gods that sit and give
The world its orders.
Give me hunger, pain and want,
Shut me out with shame and failure
From your doors of gold and fame,
Give me your shabbiest, weariest hunger!

But leave me a little love,
A voice to speak to me in the day end,
A hand to touch me in the dark room
Breaking the long loneliness.
In the dusk of day-shapes
Blurring the sunset,
One little wandering, western star
Thrust out from the changing shores of shadow.
Let me go to the window,
Watch there the day-shapes of dusk
And wait and know the coming
Of a little love.

Carl Sandburg

248 *A Prayer*

God, is it sinful if I feel
His arms about me when I kneel
To pray. His arms that thrilled and drew
Me along paths the world's youth knew?

Or is it sin if I mistake
Eternity for time—and break

One instant from the dust of years
To mix with ecstasy, and tears?

God, oh my God, the way is long
Alone. Can it be very wrong
To dream of ways I did not tread?
To weep for words I never said?

Mary Dixon Thayer

249 *Since Thou Hast Given Me This Good Hope, O God*

Since thou hast given me this good hope, O God,
That while my footsteps tread the flowery sod
And the great woods embower me, and white dawn
And purple even sweetly lead me on
From day to day and night to night, O God,
My life shall no wise miss the light of love,
But ever climbing, climb above
Man's one poor star, man's supine lands,
Into the azure steadfastness of death.
My life shall no wise lack the light of love,
My hands not lack the loving touch of hands,
But day by day, while yet I draw my breath,
And day by day unto my last of years,
I shall be one that has a perfect friend,
Her heart shall taste my laughter and my tears,
And her kind eyes shall lead me to the end.

Robert Louis Stevenson

250 *The Housewife*

Jesus, teach me how to be
Proud of my simplicity.

Sweep the floors, wash the clothes,
Gather for each vase a rose.

Iron and mend a tiny frock,
Keeping one eye on the clock.

Always having time kept free
For childish questions asked of me.

Grant me wisdom Mary had
When she taught her little Lad.

Catherine Cate Coblentz

251

The Folded Flock[1]

I saw the shepherd fold the sheep,
With all the little lambs that leap.

O Shepherd Lord, so I would be
Folded with all my family.

Or go they early, come they late,
Their mother and I must count them eight.

And how, for us, were any Heaven
If we, sorestricken, saw but seven?

Kind Shepherd, as of old Thou'lt run
And fold at need a straggling one.

Wilfrid Meynell

252

The Man's Prayer

When all is still within these walls,
And Thy sweet sleep through darkness falls
On little hearts that trust in me,
However bitter toil may be,
For length of days, O Lord! on Thee,
My spirit calls.

[1] One of the eight children of Alice and Wilfrid Meynell died within a few hours of his birth.

Their daily need by day enthralls
My hand and brain, but when night falls
And leaves the questioning spirit free
To brood upon the days to be,
For time and strength, O Lord! on Thee,
My spirit calls.

Thomas Augustus Daly

253

A Mother's Prayer

Father in Heaven, make me wise,
So that my gaze may never meet
A question in my children's eyes:
God keep me always kind and sweet—

And patient, too, before their need;
Let each vexation know its place,
Let gentleness be all my creed,
Let laughter live upon my face!

A mother's day is very long,
There are so many things to do!
But never let me lose my song
Before the hardest day is through.

Margaret E. Sangster

254

A Birthday Prayer

Keep this little light, O Father,
Burning year on year—
Driving back the dark about it
With its rays of cheer.

Keep these little feet, O Father,
Standing here to-day
By the side of life's first mile-stone,
Always in Thy way.

Keep this little heart, O Father,
Loving, pure, and true,
That when come the evening shadows
Naught shall be to rue.

Keep this little one, O Father,
Near me through life's task—
In His name, who blessed the children,
This I humbly ask.

John Finley

255 *Prayer for a Play House*

Sunshine, come softly here,
Breezes, be mild.
Rain, stay your ravages;
Dreams of a child,
Fragile and delicate
Past all repair
Beg you for clemency:
Nature, take care!

Elinor Lennan

256 *A Prayer for My Son*

Eternal Spirit, you
Whose will maintains the world,
Who thought and made it true;
The honey-suckle curled
Through the arbutus limb,
The leaves that move in air,
Are half akin to him
Whose conscious moving stare
Is drawn, yet stirs by will;
Whose little fingers bend,
Unbend, and then are still,

While the mind seeks an end.
At moments, like a vine,
He clambers through small boughs;
Then poised and half divine,
He waits with lifted brows.
To steep the mind in sense,
Yet never lose the aim,
Will make the world grow dense,
Yet by this way we came.
Earth and mind are not one,
But they are so entwined,
That this, my little son,
May yet one day go blind.
Eternal Spirit, you
Who guided Socrates,
Pity this small and new
Bright soul on hands and knees.

Yvor Winters

257 *Prayer*

God, listen through my words to the beating of my heart.
My words cry out: "Where'er Thou art,
Lift up Thine hand to guard my son;
Take not his life until his years are run.
From all disaster on the sea,
From shell and fire on land,
Protect him. Thine the gracious hand
To guide him home to me."
But deeper than my words, O Lord,
More vital than my breath,
More sure than homing birds, O Lord,
More sharp than stinging death,
The cry that knows no rest:
"Use him—Thou knowest best.
Thine the inscrutable will."
My words grow still . . .

And in the silence here at last I feel
Thy hand upon me, as I kneel.

Margueritte Harmon Bro

258

Blessing on Little Boys

God, bless all little boys who look like Puck,
  With wide eyes, wider mouths and stick-out ears.
Rash little boys who stay alive by luck
  And Heaven's favor in this world of tears,
Ten-thousand-question-asking little boys,
  Rapid of hand and foot and thought as well,
Playing with gorgeous fancies more than toys,
  Heroes in what they dream, but never tell;
Father, in your vast playground let them know
  The loveliness of ocean, star and hill;
Protect from every bitterness and woe
  Your heedless little acolytes, and still
Grant me the grace, I beg upon my knees,
Not to forget that I was one of these.

Arthur Guiterman

259

The Toys

My little Son, who look'd from thoughtful eyes
And moved and spoke in quiet grown-up wise,
Having my law the seventh time disobey'd,
I struck him, and dismiss'd
With hard words and unkiss'd,
His Mother, who was patient, being dead.
Then, fearing lest his grief should hinder sleep,
I visited his bed,
But found him slumbering deep,
With darken'd eyelids, and their lashes yet
From his late sobbing wet.
And I, with moan,

Kissing away his tears, left others of my own;
For, on a table drawn beside his head,
He had put, within his reach,
A box of counters and a red-vein'd stone,
A piece of glass abraded by the beach
And six or seven shells,
A bottle with bluebells
And two French copper coins, ranged there with careful art,
To comfort his sad heart.
So when that night I pray'd
To God, I wept, and said:
Ah, when at last we lie with tranced breath,
Not vexing Thee in death,
And Thou rememberest of what toys
We made our joys,
How weakly understood,
Thy great commanded good,
Then, fatherly not less
Than I whom Thou hast moulded from the clay
Thou'lt leave Thy wrath, and say,
"I will be sorry for their childishness."

Coventry Patmore

VII

GOD'S FAR-RANGING KINGDOM

1 · THE HOUSE OF THE ETERNAL

260 *How Amiable Are Thy Tabernacles!*

Thou, whose unmeasured temple stands,
  Built over earth and sea,
Accept the walls that human hands
  Have raised, oh God! to thee.

And let the Comforter and Friend,
  Thy Holy Spirit, meet
With those who here in worship bend
  Before thy mercy seat.

May they who err be guided here
  To find the better way,
And they who mourn and they who fear
  Be strengthened as they pray.

May faith grow firm, and love grow warm,
  And hallowed wishes rise,
While round these peaceful walls the storm
  Of earth-born passion dies.

William Cullen Bryant

261 From *The Hind and the Panther*

But, gratious God, how well dost thou provide
For erring judgments an unerring Guide!
Thy throne is darkness in th' abyss of light,
A blaze of glory that forbids the sight;
O teach me to believe Thee thus conceal'd,
And search no farther than Thy self reveal'd;

But her alone for my Directour take
Whom Thou hast promis'd never to forsake!
My thoughtless youth was wing'd with vain desires,
My manhood, long misled by wandring fires,
Follow'd false lights; and when their glimpse was gone,
My pride struck out new sparkles of her own.
Such was I, such by nature still I am,
Be Thine the glory and be mine the shame.

John Dryden

262 *Prayer in a Country Church*

I went to worship in a house of God,
Built with the loving hands and sturdy brawn
Of those who fought the forest, turned the sod,
And planted here a nation; and the dawn
That saw the springing of the pregnant seed
Seemed close: I saw the rugged, tight-lipped men
And shrinking women kneel to tell their need
And their despair, and pray for strength again.

Dear God, who tempered forces that they fought,
And filled their church and land with hallowed peace,
Send peace to men; the peace that faith has wrought
Into these walls, give to the world, nor cease
To answer ancient prayers, and ours, as again,
We pray for "peace on earth, good will to men."

Ruth B. Van Dusen

263 *A Communion Hymn*

How sweet and silent is the place,
My God, alone with thee!
Awaiting here thy touch of grace,
Thy heavenly mystery.

So many ways thou hast, dear Lord,
  My longing heart to fill:
Thy lovely world, thy spoken word,
  The doing thy sweet will.

Giving thy children living bread,
  Leading thy weak ones on,
The touch of dear hands on my head,
  The thought of loved ones gone.

Lead me by many paths, dear Lord,
  But always in thy way,
And let me make my earth a Heaven
  Till next Communion Day.

Alice Freeman Palmer

264 From *This Do in Remembrance of Me*

Here, O my Lord, I see Thee face to face;
  Here would I touch and handle things unseen,
Here grasp with firmer hand the eternal grace,
  And all my weariness upon Thee lean.

Here would I feed upon the bread of God,
  Here drink with Thee the royal wine of heaven;
Here would I lay aside each earthly load,
  Here taste afresh the calm of sin forgiven.

This is the hour of banquet and of song,
  This is the heavenly table spread for me;
Here let me feast, and, feasting, still prolong
  The brief, bright hour of fellowship with Thee.

Too soon we rise; the symbols disappear;
  The feast, though not the love, is past and gone;
The bread and wine remove, but Thou art here,
  Nearer than ever, still my Shield and Sun.

I have no help but Thine; nor do I need
Another arm save Thine to lean upon;
It is enough, my Lord, enough indeed;
My strength is in Thy might, Thy might alone.

Horatius Bonar

265

Put Forth, O God, Thy Spirit's Might

Put forth, O God, Thy Spirit's might
And bid Thy Church increase
In breadth and length, in depth and height,
Her unity and peace.

Let works of darkness disappear
Before Thy conquering light;
Let hatred and tormenting fear
Pass with the passing night.

Let what Apostles learned of Thee
Be ours from age to age;
Their steadfast faith our unity,
Their peace our heritage.

O Judge divine of human strife!
O Vanquisher of pain!
To know Thee is eternal life,
To serve Thee is to reign.

Howard Chandler Robbins

266

Laid on Thine Altar

Laid on thine altar, O my Lord divine,
Accept this gift today for Jesus' sake;
I have no jewels to adorn thy shrine,
No far-famed sacrifice to make;
But here within my trembling hand I bring

This will of mine—a thing that seemeth small.
But thou alone, O Lord, canst understand
How when I yield thee this, I yield mine all.

Hidden within, thy searching gaze can see
Struggles of passion, visions of delight,
All that I have or am or fain would be—
Deep loves, fond hopes, and longings infinite.
It has been wet with tears and hushed with sighs,
Crushed in my grasp till beauty it hath none;
Now from thy footstool where it vanquished lies,
The prayer ascendeth, "May thy will be done."

Take it, O Father, ere my courage fail,
And merge it so in thine own will, that e'en
If in some desperate hour my cries prevail
And thou give back my gift it may have been
So changed, so purified, so fair have grown,
So one with thee, so filled with grace divine,
I may not feel or know it as my own,
But, gaining back my will, may find it thine.

Author Unknown

267

A Prayer for a Preacher

If through my perjured lips Thy voice may speak,
If through a sinner Thou canst save from sin,
Go forth, my Savior, through my words to seek
And bring Thy lost ones in.

I offer Thee my hands with recent scars,
Raw with the wounds deep-cut by gyves of sin,
Ply them in prison souls to break the bars
And by me, Lord, pass in.

Edward Shillito

268 ## *Other Sheep I Have, Which Are Not of This Fold*

Look from the sphere of endless day,
  Oh, God of mercy and of might!
In pity look on those who stray,
  Benighted, in this land of light.

In peopled vale, in lonely glen,
  In crowded mart by stream or sea,
How many of the sons of men
  Hear not the message sent from thee.

Send forth thy heralds, Lord, to call
  The thoughtless young, the hardened old,
A wandering flock, and bring them all
  To the Good Shepherd's peaceful fold.

Send them thy mighty word to speak
  Till faith shall dawn and doubt depart,—
To awe the bold, to stay the weak,
  And bind and heal the broken heart.

Then all these wastes, a dreary scene,
  On which, with sorrowing eyes, we gaze,
Shall grow with living waters green,
  And lift to heaven the voice of praise.

William Cullen Bryant

269 ## *Idols*

They made them idols in the elder days,
  Idols and images of brass and stone,
To bow before their semblance, when the praise
  Should go, O God, to Thee and Thee alone.

Yet who shall say how much of tender trust,
  Of deep-heart adoration and desire
Was hid behind these symbols of the dust
  That rose like smoke to dim the central fire?

How often, in those heathen hearts, indeed,
  Ardent and upwardly there must have burned
A flame of worship, an imperious need
  To clasp and kiss the thing toward which they yearned.

Midst of the mystic Orient today,
  Far in the north, or where the great South Seas
Circle the islands, gather still to pray
  The myriad folk whose faith is like to these.

Rebuke them not: even as a root at birth
  Feels upward to the light, these simple men
Foredream the flower and darkly from the earth
  Salute the mystery beyond their ken.

Richard Burton

270

Pentecost

Fulfill, O gracious God, to-day,
  Thy promise made long ages since:
All flesh shall share the Spirit's sway,
  The young, the old, the poor, the prince.

Why delve we in a hoary past,
  For footprints of thy stately tread?
Why hear no more, in all the vast,
  The Voice that wakes the living dead?

The Vision granted but to age,
  Grant thou to youth, of courage strong;
So shall be writ a glory-page,
  In righting every human wrong.

The Spirit's power outpour, we pray,
Upon all flesh, sin-blind and lost;
Touch every soul with his bright ray,
Make every day a Pentecost.

Adelbert Sumpter Coats

271 *Eternal God Whose Searching Eye Doth Scan*

Eternal God whose searching eye doth scan
Ages and climes no limits can confine,
Broaden Thy vistas in the eyes of man
'Till he shall share the vision that is Thine.

Help him to see the Kingdom of Thy Son
Wider than nation, deeper still than race;
Chasten his joy in meager vict'ries won,
Stablish his goings in a broader place.

Lengthen the Light that shines upon his day;
Gird with Thy love the weakness of his creeds;
Teach him to trust his fellows in the Way,
Give him the faith that conquers and concedes.

Strike from his soul the fetters of his fears,
Level the barriers of the narrow mind;
Forward Thy church throughout the coming years
Wide as the world and broad as humankind.

Edwin McNeill Poteat

272 *The Prophecy Sublime*

Thy kingdom come, O Lord,
Wide-circling as the sun;
Fulfil of old thy word
And make the nations one:

One in the bond of peace,
  The service glad and free
Of truth and righteousness,
  Of love and equity.

Speed, speed the longed-for time
  Foretold by raptured seers,—
The prophecy sublime,
  The hope of all the years:

Till rise in ordered plan
  On firm foundation broad
The commonwealth of man,
  The City of our God!

Frederick L. Hosmer

2 · THIS LAND WE LOVE

273 *Invocation*

O Thou whose equal purpose runs
In drops of rain or streams of suns,
And with a soft compulsion rolls
The green earth on her snowy poles;
O Thou who keepest in thy ken
The times of flowers, the dooms of men,
Stretch out a mighty wing above—
Be tender to the land we love!

If all the huddlers from the storm
Have found her hearthstone wide and warm;
If she has made men free and glad,
Sharing, with all, the good she had;
If she has blown the very dust
From her bright balance to be just,
Oh, spread a mighty wing above—
Be tender to the land we love!

When in the dark eternal tower
The star-clock strikes her trial hour,
And for her help no more avail
Her sea-blue shield, her mountain mail,
But sweeping wide, from Gulf to Lakes,
The battle on her forehead breaks,
Throw Thou a thunderous wing above—
Be lightning for the land we love!

Wendell Phillips Stafford

274 *Hymn to the West*

O Thou, whose glorious orbs on high
  Engird the earth with splendor round,
From out thy secret place draw nigh
  The courts and temples of this ground;
    Eternal Light,
    Fill with thy might
  These domes that in thy purpose grew,
  And lift a nation's heart anew!

Illumine Thou each pathway here,
  To show the marvels God hath wrought!
Since first thy people's chief and seer
  Looked up with that prophetic thought,
    Bade Time unroll
    The fateful scroll,
  And empire unto Freedom gave
  From cloudland height to tropic wave.

Poured through the gateways of the North
  Thy mighty rivers join their tide,
And, on the wings of morn sent forth,
  Their mists the far-off peaks divide.
    By Thee unsealed,
    The mountains yield
  Ores that the wealth of Ophir shame,
  And gems enwrought of seven-hued flame.

Lo, through what years the soil hath lain
  At thine own time to give increase—
The greater and the lesser grain,
  The ripening boll, the myriad fleece!
    Thy creatures graze
    Appointed ways;
  League after league across the land
  The ceaseless herds obey thy hand.

Thou, whose high archways shine most clear
Above the plenteous Western plain,
Thine ancient tribes from round the sphere
To breathe its quickening air are fain:
And smiles the sun
To see made one
Their blood throughout Earth's greenest space,
Land of the new and lordlier race!

Edmund Clarence Stedman

275 *Lord, While for All Mankind*

Lord, while for all mankind we pray,
Of every clime and coast,
O hear us for our native land,
The land we love the most.

O guard our shores from every foe;
With peace our borders bless,
Our cities with prosperity,
Our field with plenteousness.

Unite us in the sacred love
Of knowledge, truth, and Thee;
And let our hills and valleys shout
The songs of liberty.

Lord of the nations, thus to Thee
Our country we commend;
Be Thou her refuge and her trust,
Her everlasting Friend.

John R. Wreford

276 *Wanted*

God give us men! A time like this demands
Strong minds, great hearts, true faith, and ready hands;

Men whom the lust of office does not kill;
  Men whom the spoils of office cannot buy;
Men who possess opinions and a will;
  Men who have honor,—men who will not lie;
Men who can stand before a demagogue,
  And damn his treacherous flatteries without winking!
Tall men, sun-crowned, who live above the fog
  In public duty, and in private thinking:
For while the rabble, with their thumb-worn creeds,
Their large professions and their little deeds,—
Mingle in selfish strife, lo! Freedom weeps,
Wrong rules the land, and waiting Justice sleeps.

Josiah Gilbert Holland

277 From *Hymn*

God of the strong, God of the weak,
  Lord of all lands, and our own land;
Light of all souls, from Thee we seek
  Light from Thy light, strength from Thy hand.

In suffering Thou hast made us one,
  In mighty burdens one are we;
Teach us that lowliest duty done
  Is highest service unto Thee.

Teach us, Great Teacher of mankind,
  The sacrifice that brings Thy balm;
The love, the work that bless and bind;
  Teach us Thy majesty, Thy calm.

Teach Thou, and we shall know, indeed,
  The truth divine that maketh free;
And knowing, we may sow the seed
  That blossoms through eternity;—

May sow in every living heart
  That to the waiting day doth ope.
Not ours, O God! the craven part,
  To shut one human soul from hope.

Richard Watson Gilder

3 · THROUGH WAR TO PEACE

278 *God of the Nations*

God of the Nations, who from dawn of days
Hast led Thy people in their widening ways,
Through whose deep purpose stranger thousands stand
Here in the borders of our promised land;

Thine ancient might rebuked the Pharaoh's boast,
Thou wast the shield for Israel's marching host,
And, all the ages through, past crumbling throne
And broken fetter, Thou hast brought Thine own.

Thy hand has led across the hungry sea
The eager peoples flocking to be free,
And from the breeds of earth, Thy silent sway
Fashions the Nation of the broadening day.

Then, for Thy grace to grow in brotherhood
For hearts aflame to serve Thy destined good,
For faith, and will to win what faith shall see,
God of Thy people, hear us cry to Thee!

Walter Russell Bowie

279 *Prayer during Battle*

Lord, in this day of battle,
  Lord, in this night of fears,
Keep open, oh, keep open
  My eyes, my ears.

Not blindly, not in hatred,
  Lord, let me do my part.

Keep open, oh, keep open
My mind, my heart!
Hermann Hagedorn

280 *A Soldier's Prayer*

White Captain of my soul, lead on;
I follow Thee, come dark or dawn.
Only vouchsafe three things I crave:
Where terror stalks, help me be brave!
Where righteous ones can scarce endure
The siren call, help me be pure!
Where vows grow dim, and men dare do
What once they scorned, help me be true!
Robert Freeman

281 *Invocation*

There is no balm on earth:
Nothing but strife and din.
Relieve us of our dearth,
Spirit of Peace within!

Across the sky there dart
Monsters of strident wing;
But still within the heart
The quiet birds may sing.

What sheaves are these we bind?
The fields are rank with doom.
But still within the mind
The seed may freshly bloom.

The flames of chaos roll,
Mocking our dazed replies;

But still within the soul
  May healing waters rise.

All outward spells are vain
  The victory to win.
Stir! Quicken us again,
  Spirit of Life within!
Gilbert Thomas

282 *The Fallen*

Those we have loved the dearest,
  The bravest and the best,
Are summoned from the battle
  To their eternal rest;

There they endure the silence,
  Here we endure the pain—
He that bestows the Valour
  Valour resumes again.

O, Master of all Being,
  Donor of Day and Night,
Of Passion and of Beauty,
  Of Sorrow and Delight,

Thou gav'st them the full treasure
  Of that heroic blend—
The Pride, the Faith, the Courage,
  That holdeth to the end.

Thou gavest us the Knowledge
  Wherein their memories stir—
Master of Life, we thank Thee
  That they were what they were.
Duncan Campbell Scott

283 *Hymnal*

Bringer of sun, arrower of evening, star-begetter and moon-riser,
Hear our prayer for peace, that the bayonet be broken;
Bringer of tide to the marshes, of fruit to wayward orchards,
Remember us who have been betrayed. Anoint the heavy spirit of man.

It is enough that the sower go forth, the plower awake at morning, remembering the furrow,
That the cock crow back day, waking the green eyelids of the trees,
Enough that man should love in the spring and feel the flint of the wind.

Giver of arbutus and rhododendron, waker of petal and tendril, reward us in this hour,
This hour of pestilence and war. Erase chaos from the mind, the heart's sour sickness.

It is enough to lie on a hill at twilight, hands locked under the boughs;
It is enough to walk by the sea, the estuary, the hill,
Content with the wind's words, the sea's washed spindrift of speech.

Bringer of night, waker of Arcturus in the heavens, driver of Aurora's chariot,
Be with us now. Give us surcease from confusion.
Bringer of rain, remember the birth of magnolia, the death of the fuchsia,
Remember the faith of the earth and the holy burden of man.

Harold Vinal

284 *Give Our Conscience Light*

Shine forth into the night, O flame
Of love. The world is lost
In chaos. Heap the war-crime blame

On us till Pentecost
Will come again with tongues of fire
To burn upon our heads.
Let our last breath of greed expire
Until new vision spreads
Like waking dawn when earth began.
Oh, give us God-filled sight!
Shine forth through darkness, Son of Man,
And give our conscience light.

Aline B. Carter

285

A Prayer for Thanksgiving

We thank Thee for the joy of common things:
The laughter of a child, the vagrant grace
Of water, the great wind that beats its wings,
The sudden light that shines upon a face.

We thank Thee for the heavens that declare
Thy love, and the abundant earth no less;
We thank Thee for the bread we eat and share
From hearts that overflow with thankfulness.

We thank Thee that when we grow puffed with pride
And blurt out wild and foolish blasphemies,
The gentler angels of our nature chide,
And Thy forgiveness brings us to our knees.

Against the voices counseling despair
We thank Thee for the clarions of youth,
For humbleness that turns to Thee in prayer,
For courage that is not afraid of truth.

O Lord, we thank Thee (when no man is sleeping,
But watches, nor dares he draw quiet breath)
That, kenneled and confided to our keeping,
We guard the dreadful atom brood of death.

We thank Thee that man's spirit need not falter,
That Faith still fights the good and gallant fight,
That still the torches on the anxious altar
Of Freedom, though they flicker, burn as bright.

For strength for this day's huge and harsh demanding
We thank Thee, Lord; for patience yet to find
A brave new hope, a brave new understanding
In the vast commonwealth of heart and mind.

Lord, from the blind abyss of circumstance
Whither, by war's grim folly, we were hurled,
We thank Thee for a final golden chance
To rise again and build a nobler world.

Joseph Auslander

286 *The Prince of Peace*

The Prince of Peace, his banner spreads,
His wayward folk to lead
From war's embattled hate and dreads,
Its bulwarked ire and greed.
O marshal us, the sons of sires
Who braved the cannon's roar,
To venture all that peace requires
As they dared death for war.

Lead on, O Christ! That haunting song
No centuries can dim,
Which long ago the heavenly throng
Sang over Bethlehem.
Cast down our rancor, fear, and pride,
Exalt goodwill again!
Our worship doth thy name deride,
Bring we not peace to men.

Thy pardon, Lord, for war's dark shame,
  Its death-strewn, bloody fields!
Yet thanks to thee for souls aflame
  Who dared with swords and shields!
O Christ, who died to give men life,
  Bring that victorious hour,
When man shall use for peace, not strife,
  His valor, skill, and power.

Cleanse all our hearts from our disgrace—
  We love not world, but clan!
Make clear our eyes to see our race
  One family of man.
Rend thou our little temple veils
  That cloak the truth divine,
Until thy mighty word prevails,
  That cries, 'All souls are mine.'

Harry Emerson Fosdick

287

Clean Hands

Make this thing plain to us, O Lord!
That not the triumph of the sword—
  Not that alone—can end the strife,
  But reformation of the life—
But full submission to Thy Word!

Not all the stream of blood outpoured
Can Peace—the Long-Desired—afford;
  Not tears of Mother, Maid or Wife . . .
    Make this thing plain!

We must root out our sins ignored,
By whatsoever name adored;
  Our secret sins, that, ever rife,
  Shrink from the operating knife;

Then shall we rise, renewed, restored . . .
Make this thing plain!

Austin Dobson

288

Prayer for Light

When children, blundering on their fathers' guns,
Brandish the murderous loot in screaming play,
There is a chance, before the live blood runs,
That older hands may snatch the tools away.
But ah, when man hacks down his wharves and towers,
Groping with toys that shame the whirlwind's force,
Who shall redeem the child? what sterner powers
Shall save him from his own cyclonic course?

O Wisdom of the Timeless! We have need
Of guidance greater than man's brain affords,
When this torn urchin, doomed to writhe and bleed,
Sows an unreckoned fruit with bombs and swords!
He knows not what he does, nor where to go!
O grant him light to see himself as foe!

Stanton A. Coblentz

289

Prayer for the Age

God, who devisedst man who then devised
The axe, the arrow, and the armored tank,
Until his hand, which once was moderate-sized,
Increased in reach beyond his moral rank—

God, who hast smiled on razor-blades and rayon
Succeeding Neolithic flints and skins,
Give man a modern basis now to pray on—
Forgive him for his Neolithic sins.

Myron H. Broomell

290 *A Prayer from 1936*

We are souls in hell, who hear no gradual music
Advancing on the air, on wave-lengths walking.
We are lost in life, who listen for hope and hear
but
The tyrant and the politician talking.

Out of the nothingness of night they tell
Our need of guns, our servitude to strife.
O heaven of music, absolve us from this hell
Unto unmechanized mastery over life.

Siegfried Sassoon

291 From *A Prayer of the Peoples*

God of us who kill our kind!
Master of this blood-tracked Mind
Which from wolf and Caliban
Staggers toward the star of Man—
Now, on Thy cathedral stair,
God, we cry to Thee in prayer!

❈

Save us from our tribal gods!
From the racial powers, whose rods—
Wreathed with stinging serpents—stir
Odin and old Jupiter
From their ancient hells of hate
To invade Thy dawning state.

❈

We who, craven in our prayer,
Would lay off on Thee our care—
Lay instead on *us* Thy load;
On our minds Thy spirit's goad,
On our laggard wills Thy whips
And Thy passion on our lips.

Percy MacKaye

292 From *The Christ of the Andes*

O Christ of Olivet, you hushed the wars
Under the far Andean stars:
Lift now your strong nail-wounded hands
Over all peoples, over all lands:
Stretch out those comrade hands to be
A shelter over land and sea!

Edwin Markham

293 *For the Gifts of the Spirit*

Send down thy truth, O God!
Too long the shadows frown;
Too long the darkened way we've trod:
Thy truth, O Lord, send down!

Send down thy Spirit free,
Till wilderness and town
One temple for thy worship be:
Thy Spirit, oh, send down.

Send down thy love, thy life,
Our lesser lives to crown,
And cleanse them of their hate and strife:
Thy living love send down!

Send down thy peace, O Lord!
Earth's bitter voices drown
In one deep ocean of accord:
Thy peace, O God, send down!

Edward Rowland Sill

4 · THE ENLARGING BROTHERHOOD

294 *To the Christ*

Thou hast on earth a Trinity—
Thyself, my fellow-man, and me;
When one with him, then one with Thee;
Nor save together Thine are we.

John Banister Tabb

295 *Shine on Me, Secret Splendor*

Shine on me, Secret Splendor, till I feel
That all are one upon the mighty wheel.
Let me be brother to the meanest clod,
Knowing he, too, bears on the dream of God;
Yet be fastidious, and have such friends
That when I think of them my soul ascends!

Edwin Markham

296 *O Young and Fearless Prophet*

O young and fearless Prophet of ancient Galilee:
Thy life is still a summons to serve humanity,
To make our thoughts and actions less prone to please the crowd,
To stand with humble courage for thee with hearts uncowed.

We marvel at the purpose that held thee to thy course,
While ever on the hilltop before thee loomed the cross;
Thy steadfast face set forward where love and duty shone,
While we betray so quickly and leave thee there alone.

O help us stand unswerving against war's bloody way,
Where hate and lust and falsehood hold back Christ's holy sway;

Forbid such love of country as blinds us to his call
Who sets above the nation the brotherhood of all.

Create in us the splendor that dawns when hearts are kind,
That knows not race or station as boundaries of the mind;
That learns to value beauty in heart, or brain, or soul,
And longs to bind God's children into one perfect whole.

Stir up in us a protest against the greed of wealth,
While men go starved and hungry who plead for work and health;
Whose wives and little children cry out for lack of bread,
Who spend their years o'erweighted beneath a gloomy dread.

O young and fearless Prophet, we need thy presence here,
Amid our pride and glory to see thy face appear;
Once more to hear thy challenge above our noisy day,
Triumphantly to lead us along God's holy way.

S. Ralph Harlow

297 *Hymn*

Thou God of all, whose presence dwells
Within the myriad forms of earth,
Whose quickening spirit brings to birth
Atoms and stars and living cells;

Thou God, whose thought and purpose brood
On men of every coast and clime,
Whose justice falls, through changeless time,
Alike on evil and on good;

Forgive, we pray thee, our conceit
In holding thee to be our own,
Our arrogance that we alone
Receive and share thy mercy meet.

Our pride condemns us in thy sight,
Bows us beneath thy ban and bane.
The humble seek thee not in vain;
The meek are haloed by thy light.

John Haynes Holmes

298 *Prayer*

Take from the earth its tragic hunger, Lord,
And to the barren, crystalled stalk concede
This terraced wind-swept and the wingéd hoard
Of empty throats. This dearth cannot impede
The vibrant, living green regenerate
Within the root. Where now a deepened blight
Conceals the restless, molten surge of hate,
Direct a quiet miracle of Light.

Take from the heart its tragic hunger, Lord,
And with discerning grace avow thy gift
Of leaven to the slow, unkerneled wheat;
Confirm within this hour thy sacred Word;
Redeem thy parenthood, and we uplift
The hollow, famished cup of Love, replete!

Hazel J. Fowler

299 *The Litany of the Dark People*

Our flesh that was a battle-ground
Shows now the morning-break;
The ancient deities are drowned
For Thy eternal sake.
Now that the past is left behind,
Fling wide Thy garment's hem
To keep us one with Thee in mind,
Thou Christ of Bethlehem.

The thorny wreath may ridge our brow,
The spear may mar our side,
And on white wood from a scented bough
We may be crucified;
Yet no assault the old gods make
Upon our agony
Shall swerve our footsteps from the wake
Of Thine toward Calvary.

And if we hunger now and thirst,
Grant our withholders may,
When heaven's constellations burst
Upon Thy crowning day,
Be fed by us, and given to see
Thy mercy in our eyes,
When Bethlehem and Calvary
Are merged in Paradise.

Countee Cullen

300 *Almighty God, Whose Justice Like a Sun*

Almighty God, whose justice like a sun
Shall coruscate along the floors of Heaven,
Raising what's low, perfecting what's undone,
Breaking the proud and making odd things even.
The poor of Jesus Christ along the street
In your rain sodden, in your snows unshod,
They have nor hearth, nor sword, nor human meat,
Nor even the bread of men: Almighty God.

The poor of Jesus Christ whom no man hears
Have waited on your vengeance much too long.
Wipe out not tears but blood: our eyes bleed tears.
Come smite our damnéd sophistries so strong
That thy rude hammer battering this rude wrong
Ring down the abyss of twice ten thousand years.

Hilaire Belloc

301 *The Common Lot*

Grant me to share the common, human lot.
I ask not, Lord, that Thou remit a jot
Of pain, and granting joy, forget me not!

Have I not known the sweetest human bliss,
That angels envy, just a loving kiss?
Why should I ask then not to hear the hiss

Of serpents walking round in human guise,
The stab of envy, and the sad surprise
Of reputation blackened by surmise?

Of One we read: In Him we ever see
The dew of Youth, and: Perfected was He
By suffering consummated on the tree!

A lesser one, his servant, boasts his joy,
And tribulation too in high employ,
Made great by gladness and by deep annoy.

In sorrow, yet rejoicing evermore;
As poor, but riches adding to the score—
Repeated contradiction, o'er and o'er!

Blind Homer, and blind Milton greatly please.
Only the eye God-blinded ever sees;
And eloquence is borne with mute Demosthenes.

Nay, no one can nobility attain
Who knoweth not the sum of human pain,
And regal gladness both of heart and brain.

No picture beautiful can artist paint
Save light and shadow meet in sweet constraint;
Life is a web of deep content and plaint.

How shall I meet and talk with those I know
In the eternities, if I forego
The joy, the woe, that made their faces glow?

Or how companion in dim distant years
With those who serve and reign in other spheres,
Made great through mighty laughter and hot tears?

Nay let me fare with those who loyally
Have lived the life complex—a symphony
Of highest joy and deepest agony!

Adelbert Sumpter Coats

302 *A Prayer for Charity*

Because I do not always know
Of hidden thorns that goad the flesh
Beneath the mask of face and dress,
I shall deal gently as I go.

Because I do not always see,
Under quick words or sudden stress,
The sting of some lost happiness,
I shall essay true charity.

Always, dear Lord, I ask a mind
That does not need a spear-torn side
Or sight of body crucified
To teach me not to be unkind.

Edwin O. Kennedy

303 *O Mind of God, Broad as the Sky*

O mind of God, broad as the sky,
The earth, the air, the sea,
Give us thy broad'ning Spirit's grace,
In sweet simplicity.

O heart of God, deep as the needs
Of all humanity,
Give unto us the kindlier soul,
The larger sympathy.

O will of God, high as all heav'n
With pow'r superb and free,
Give us the will to do and dare,
In fullest liberty.

O large and free and glorious God,
With ways exceeding kind,
Give unto us thy breadth of love,
In loving all mankind.

Oliver Huckel

304

A Prayer

O Love, give me a passionate heart
That my heart may be pure.
Give me, O Love, thy harder part,
The daring to endure.
Lead me not in ways too green
Lest my faith cease to strive,
Keep thou thy sword for ever keen
To stab my soul alive.
O give me thy deep strength to hold
Thy peace within my breast,
All sick and sorrowing hearts to fold
In thy enfolding rest.

Irene Rutherford McLeod

305

A Prayer

Until I lose my soul and lie
Blind to the beauty of the earth,
Deaf though a shouting wind goes by,
Dumb in a storm of mirth;

Until my heart is quenched at length
And I have left the land of men,
Oh, let me love with all my strength
Careless if I am loved again.

Sara Teasdale

306 From *Invocation*

Empty my heart, Lord, of daily vices;
Anxiety, conversation, and selfish prayer;
Teach me to know each minute its own crisis,
And make my views of other men not theirs.
Wipe from my mind, Lord, the inner smirk
That swells from lack of love's humility;
Empty me of myself, that when I work,
All that I work for, never concerns me.

Theodore Spencer

307 *Prayer before Study*

Constricted by my tortured thought,
I am too centred on this spot.

So caged and cadged, so close within
A coat of unessential skin,

I would put off myself and flee
My inaccessibility.

A fool can play at being solemn
Revolving on his spinal column.

Deliver me, O Lord, from all
Activity centripetal.

Theodore Roethke

308 From *Epilogue*

Giver of bliss and pain, of song and prayer,
Thou God that dost demand
Single allegiance of the soul that sees
Thee dual only and at enmity—
Hearken my choice, my supplication hark.
Tear out the rapture and the wings—
Take back thy gift of song—
Take, take the madness of the olive and the vine
With all their ecstasies, unless they be
Not oil for gleaming of the games and clustered gold,
Not wine for leafy laughter of the feast,
But aid and chrismed healing for the wounds
Of them that smitten lie on that broad way
Known to the dusty sandals from Samaria.
Crush Thou, O God, the petalled crimson of my life,
So Thou but mold the remnant clay
To shape not all unworthy of the Thee in me.

William Alexander Percy

309 *Because of Thy Great Bounty*

Because I have been given much,
I, too, must give:
Because of Thy great bounty, Lord,
Each day I live
I shall divide my gifts from Thee
With every brother that I see
Who has the need of help from me.

Because I have been sheltered, fed,
By Thy good care,
I cannot see another's lack
And I not share

My glowing fire, my loaf of bread,
My roof's safe shelter overhead,
That he, too, may be comforted.

Because love has been lavished so
Upon me, Lord,
A wealth I know that was not meant
For me to hoard,
I shall give love to those in need,
Shall show that love by word and deed,
Thus shall my thanks be thanks indeed.

Grace Noll Crowell

310 *The Need*

Nobody knows
Whither our delirium of invention goes,
Who turn toward time to come
Alone with heart-beats, marching to that muffled drum.
Nobody hears
Bells from beyond the silence of the years
That wait for those unborn.
O God within me, speak from your mysterious morn.

Speak, through the few,
Your light of life to nourish us anew.
Speak, for our world possessed
By demon influences of evil and unrest.
Act, as of old,
That we some dawnlit destiny may behold
From this doom-darkened place.
O move in mercy among us. Grant accepted grace.

Siegfried Sassoon

311 *Prayer against Indifference*

When wars and ruined men shall cease
To vex my body's house of peace,

And bloody children lying dead
Let me lie softly in my bed
To nurse a whole and sacred skin,
Break roof and let the bomb come in.

Knock music at the templed skull
And say the world is beautiful,
But never let the dweller lock
Its house against another knock;
Never shut out the gun, the scream,
Never lie blind within a dream.

Within these walls the brain shall sit
And chew on life surrounding it;
Eat the soft sunlight hour and then
The bitter taste of bleeding men;
But never underneath the sun
Shall it forget the scream, the gun.

Let me have eyes I need not shut;
Let me have truth at my tongue's root;
Let courage and the brain command
The honest fingers of my hand;
And when I wait to save my skin
Break roof and let my death come in.

Joy Davidman

312 *Hymn*

Eternal Ruler of the ceaseless round
Of circling planets singing on their way;
Guide of the nations from the night profound
Into the glory of the perfect day;
Rule in our hearts, that we may ever be
Guided, and strengthened, and upheld by Thee.

We are of Thee, the children of Thy love,
  The brothers of Thy well-beloved Son;
Descend, O Holy Spirit, like a dove,
  Into our hearts, that we may be as one;
As one with Thee, to whom we ever tend,
As one with Him, our brother and our friend.

We would be one in hatred of all wrong,
  One in our love of all things sweet and fair,
One with the joy that breaketh into song,
  One with the grief that trembles into prayer,
One in the power that makes Thy children free
To follow truth, and thus to follow Thee.

Oh, clothe us with Thy heavenly armor, Lord!
  Thy trusty shield, Thy sword of love divine;
Our inspiration be Thy constant word,
  We ask no victories that are not Thine;
Give or withhold, let pain or pleasure be,
Enough to know that we are serving Thee.

John W. Chadwick

313 *A Hymn*

O God of earth and altar,
  Bow down and hear our cry,
Our earthly rulers falter,
  Our people drift and die;
The walls of gold entomb us,
  The swords of scorn divide,
Take not thy thunder from us,
  But take away our pride.

From all that terror teaches,
  From lies of tongue and pen,
From all the easy speeches
  That comfort cruel men,

For sale and profanation
   Of honor and the sword,
From sleep and from damnation,
   Deliver us, good Lord.

Tie in a living tether
   The prince and priest and thrall,
Bind all our lives together,
   Smite us and save us all;
In ire and exultation
   Aflame with faith, and free,
Lift up a living nation,
   A single sword to thee.

Gilbert Keith Chesterton

VIII

DISCIPLINES OF THE SPIRITUAL LIFE

1 · TOWARD FULLNESS OF LIFE

314

Would That I Were

Would that I were,—O hear thy suppliant, thou,
  Whom fond belief still ventures here to see,—
Would that I were not that which I am now
  Nor yet became the thing I wish to be!
What wouldst thou? Poor suggestion of today
  Depart, vain fancy and fallacious thought!
Would I could wish my wishes all away,
  And learn to wish the wishes that I ought.

Arthur Hugh Clough

315

Show Me Thyself

When the waves of trouble roll
O'er the weary, burdened soul,
Saviour, I shall strengthened be,
If Thou show Thyself to me!

When the sun of joy is bright,
And I revel in its light,
Lest earth's bliss too dazzling be,
Manifest Thyself to me!

When I wander from the way,
In the paths of danger stray,
Bending down in mercy free,
Saviour, show Thyself to me!

Spirit, Comforter divine!
Be my heart Thy blessed shrine!

From the tempter's snares set free,
Come and show Thyself to me!

While earth's suns and shadows meet,
Mingling round my pilgrim feet,
Till in heaven I rest with Thee,
Saviour, show Thyself to me!

Margaret E. Sangster

316 *The Contrite Heart*

The Lord will happiness divine
  On contrite hearts bestow;
Then tell me, gracious God, is mine
  A contrite heart or no?

I hear, but seem to hear in vain,
  Insensible as steel;
If aught is felt, 'tis only pain,
  To find I cannot feel.

I sometimes think myself inclined
  To love Thee if I could;
But often feel another mind,
  Averse to all that's good.

My best desires are faint and few,
  I fain would strive for more;
But when I cry, "My strength renew!"
  Seem weaker than before.

Thy saints are comforted, I know,
  And love Thy house of prayer;
I therefore go where others go,
  But find no comfort there.

Oh make this heart rejoice or ache;
  Decide this doubt for me;
And if it be not broken, break—
  And heal it, if it be.

William Cowper

317 From *The Brewing of Soma*

Dear Lord and Father of mankind,
  Forgive our foolish ways!
Reclothe us in our rightful mind,
In purer lives Thy service find,
  In deeper reverence, praise.

In simple trust like theirs who heard
  Beside the Syrian sea
The gracious calling of the Lord,
Let us, like them, without a word,
  Rise up and follow Thee.

❉

Drop Thy still dews of quietness,
  Till all our strivings cease;
Take from our souls the strain and stress,
And let our ordered lives confess
  The beauty of Thy peace.

Breathe through the heats of our desire
  Thy coolness and Thy balm;
Let sense be dumb, let flesh retire;
Speak through the earthquake, wind, and fire,
  O still, small voice of calm!

John Greenleaf Whittier

318 From *Lines Written in Kensington Gardens*

Calm soul of all things! make it mine
To feel, amid the city's jar,

That there abides a peace of thine,
Man did not make, and cannot mar.

The will to neither strive nor cry,
The power to feel with others give!
Calm, calm me more! nor let me die
Before I have begun to live.

Matthew Arnold

319

A Prayer

Lord, not for light in darkness do we pray,
Not that the veil be lifted from our eyes,
Nor that the slow ascension of our day
Be otherwise.

Not for a clearer vision of the things
Whereof the fashioning shall make us great,
Not for remission of the peril and stings
Of time and fate.

Not for a fuller knowledge of the end
Whereto we travel, bruised yet unafraid,
Nor that the little healing that we lend
Shall be repaid.

Not these, O Lord. We would not break the bars
Thy wisdom sets about us; we shall climb
Unfettered to the secrets of the stars
In Thy good time.

We do not crave the high perception swift
When to refrain were well, and when fulfil,
Nor yet the understanding strong to sift
The good from ill.

Not these, O Lord. For these Thou hast revealed,
We know the golden season when to reap
The heavy-fruited treasure of the field,
 The hour to sleep.

Not these. We know the hemlock from the rose,
The pure from stained, the noble from the base,
The tranquil holy light of truth that glows
 On Pity's face.

We know the paths wherein our feet should press,
Across our hearts are written Thy decrees,
Yet now, O Lord, be merciful to bless
 With more than these.

Grant us the will to fashion as we feel,
Grant us the strength to labour as we know,
Grant us the purpose, ribbed and edged with steel,
 To strike the blow.

Knowledge we ask not—knowledge Thou hast lent,
But, Lord, the will—there lies our bitter need,
Give us to build above the deep intent
 The deed, the deed.

John Drinkwater

320 *Thou Knowest*

Thou knowest, Thou who art the soul of all
Selfless endeavor, how I longed to make
This deed of mine, adventured for love's sake,
Thy deed—sweet grapes upon a sunny wall,
A rose whose petals into fragrance fall,
A glint of heaven glassed in some lonely lake
Amidst the heather and the fringing brake,
Our secret—ah, Thou knowest. Though it call

Only for pardon, still to Thee I bring
My poor, shamed deed that craved the beautiful,
To Thee, the Master-Artist, who alone
Wilt of Thy grace see in this graceless thing
The pattern marred by the imperfect tool,
And know that dim, wronged pattern for Thine own.

Katharine Lee Bates

321 From *Paraphrase on Thomas à Kempis*

Speak, Gracious Lord, oh speak; thy Servant hears:
  For I'm thy Servant, and I'll still be so:
Speak words of Comfort in my willing Ears;
  And since my Tongue is in thy praises slow,
And since that thine all Rhetorick exceeds;
Speak Thou in words, but let me speak in deeds!

Alexander Pope

322 *O God, in Restless Living*

O God, in restless living
We lose our spirits' peace.
Calm our unwise confusion,
Bid thou our clamor cease.
Let anxious hearts grow quiet,
Like pools at evening still,
Till thy reflected heavens
All our spirits fill.

Teach us, beyond our striving,
The rich rewards of rest.
Who does not live serenely
Is never deeply blest.
O tranquil, radiant Sunlight,
Bring thou our lives to flower,
Less wearied with our effort
More aware of power.

Receptive make our spirits,
Our need is to be still;
As dawn fades flickering candle
So dim our anxious will.
Reveal thy radiance through us,
Thine ample strength release.
Not ours but thine the triumph,
In the power of peace.

We grow not wise by struggling,
We gain but things by strain.
We cease to water gardens,
When comes thy plenteous rain.
O, beautify our spirits
In restfulness from strife;
Enrich our souls in secret
With abundant life.

Harry Emerson Fosdick

323 *Patience*

Sometimes I wish that I might do
  Just one grand deed and die,
And by that one grand deed reach up
  To meet God in the sky.
But such is not Thy way, O God,
  Not such is Thy decree,
But deed by deed, and tear by tear,
  Our souls must climb to Thee,
As climbed the only Son of God
  From manger unto Cross,
Who learned, through tears and bloody sweat,
  To count this world but loss;
Who left the Virgin Mother's Arms
  To seek those arms of shame,
Outstretched upon the lonely hill
  To which the darkness came.

As deed by deed, and tear by tear,
He climbed up to the height,
Each deed a splendid deed, each tear
A jewel shining bright,
So grant us, Lord, the patient heart,
To climb the upward way,
Until we stand upon the height,
And see the perfect day.

G. A. Studdert-Kennedy

324 *Prayer for Contentment*

Make me content, O Lord, with daily bread.
The days and weeks that crowd beyond suggest
A thousand little cares. Thou knowest best
The joys and tears that fill my path ahead.

Fill to the full my empty hands today
With service, kindness, love, humility—
Not gifts that I may *have,* but I may *be*—
Tomorrow always is a night away.

No lily languishes nor hangs her head,
No God-watched sparrow anxious quits her play
But spends the wealth of every happy day.
Make me content, O Lord, with daily bread.

Edwin McNeill Poteat

325 *A Prayer for the Old Courage*

Still let us go the way of beauty; go
The way of loveliness; still let us know
Those paths that lead where Pan and Daphne run,
Where roses prosper in the Summer sun.

The earth may rock with War. Still is there peace
In many a place to give the heart release

From this too-vibrant pain that drives men mad.
Let us go back to the old love we had.

Let us go back, to keep alive the gleam,
To cherish the immortal, God-like dream;
Not as poor cravens flying from the fight,
But as sad children seeking the clean light.

O doubly precious now is solitude;
Thrice dear yon quiet star above the wood,
Since panic and the sundering shock of War
Have laid in ruins all we hungered for.

Brave soldiers of the spirit, guard ye well
Mountain and fort and massive citadel;
But keep ye white forever—keep ye whole
The battlements of dream within the soul!

Charles Hanson Towne

326 *The Thoughts That Move the Heart of Man*

The thoughts that move the heart of man
  And lift his soul on high;
The skill that teaches him to plan
  With wondrous subtlety,—

These are thy thoughts, Almighty Mind,
  This skill is thine, O Lord,
Who dost by hidden influence bind
  All powers in sweet accord.

O fill us now, thou living Power,
  With energy divine;
Thus shall our wills from hour to hour
  Become not ours, but thine.

Ebenezer S. Oakley

2 · HE SHALL DIRECT THY PATHS

327 *The Lowest Place*

Give me the lowest place; not that I dare
  Ask for that lowest place, but Thou hast died
That I might live and share
  Thy glory by Thy side.

Give me the lowest place: or if for me
  That lowest place too high, make one more low
Where I may sit and see
  My God and love Thee so.

Christina G. Rossetti

328 *Prayer*

Lord, as thou wilt, bestow,
Light ease or heavy bearing,
Still shall my day be sharing
Thy bounty's overflow.

Thy mercy oppress me;
Thy temperance bless me;
Lord, sternly or sweetly,
Employ me discreetly,
That peace may possess me.

Eduard Mörike
Tr. John Drinkwater

329 *With Self Dissatisfied*

Not when, with self dissatisfied,
  O Lord, I lowly lie,

So much I need thy grace to guide,
  And thy reproving eye,—

As when the sound of human praise
  Grows pleasant to my ear,
And in its light my broken ways
  Fair and complete appear.

By failure and defeat made wise,
  We come to know at length
What strength within our weakness lies,
  What weakness in our strength:

What inward peace is born of strife,
  What power, of being spent;
What wings unto our upward life
  Is noble discontent.

O Lord, we need thy shaming look
  That burns all low desire;
The discipline of thy rebuke
  Shall be refining fire!

Frederick L. Hosmer

330 *Christian Freedom*

Make me a captive, Lord,
  And then I shall be free;
Force me to render up my sword,
  And I shall conqueror be;
I sink in life's alarms
  When by myself I stand;
Imprison me within Thy arms,
  And strong shall be my hand.

My power is faint and low
  Till I have learned to serve;

It wants the needed fire to glow,
  It wants the breeze to nerve;
It cannot drive the world
  Until itself be driven;
Its flag can only be unfurled
  When Thou shalt breathe from heaven.

My heart is weak and poor
  Until it master find:
It has no spring of action sure,
  It varies with the wind:
It cannot freely move
  Till thou hast wrought its chain;
Enslave it with thy matchless love,
  And deathless it shall reign.

My will is not my own
  Till Thou hast made it Thine;
If it would reach a monarch's throne
  It must its crown resign;
It only stands unbent
  Amid the clashing strife,
When on Thy bosom it has leant
  And found in Thee its life.

George Matheson

331 *Holy Sonnet XIV*

Batter my heart, three person'd God; for, you
As yet but knocke, breathe, shine, and seeke to mend;
That I may rise, and stand, o'erthrow mee, and bend
Your force, to breake, blowe, burn and make me new.
I, like an usurpt towne, to another due,
Labour to admit you, but Oh, to no end,
Reason your viceroy in mee, mee should defend,
But is captiv'd, and proves weake or untrue.
Yet dearly I love you, and would be loved faine,

But am betroth'd unto your enemie:
Divorce mee, untie, or breake that knot againe,
Take mee to you, imprison mee, for I
Except you enthrall me, never shall be free,
Nor ever chast, except you ravish mee.

John Donne

332 *Deo Optimo Maximo*

All else for use, One only for desire;
Thanksgiving for the good, but thirst for Thee:
Up from the best, whereof no man need tire,
Impel Thou me.

Delight is menace if Thou brood not by,
Power is a quicksand, Fame a gathering jeer.
Oft as the morn (though none of earth deny
These three are dear),

Wash me of them, that I may be renewed,
And wander free amid my freeborn joys:
Oh, close my hand upon Beatitude!
Not on her toys.

Louise Imogen Guiney

333 *Supplication*

I do not ask Thee straightway to appear,
But that my wall be down, my pathway clear,
The passions emptied that my heart have blocked,
My mind unguarded and my soul unlocked.

I do not ask one gem of Thy rich blood,
One petal from the tree of life in bud,
One drop of all Thy body's flowering balm,
But that I hold it, though it burn my palm.

I do not ask Thee to reveal Thy face
And all the darkness of the night displace,
But that mine eyes be equal to the day.
For this I pray. For this alone I pray.

Edith Lovejoy Pierce

334

Petition

O Lord, I pray: that for each happiness
My housemate brings I may give back no less
Than all my fertile will;

That I may take from friends but as the stream
Creates again the hawthorn bloom adream
Above the river sill;

That I may see the spurge upon the wall
And hear the nesting birds give call to call,
Keeping my wonder new;

That I may have a body fit to mate
With the green fields, the stars, and streams in spate,
And clean as clover-dew;

That I may have the courage to confute
All fools with silence when they will dispute,
All fools who will deride;

That I may know all strict and sinewy art
As that in man which is the counterpart,
Lord, of Thy fiercest pride;

That somehow this beloved earth may wear
A later grace for all the love I bear,
For some song that I sing;

That, when I die, this word may stand for me—
He had a heart to praise, an eye to see,
And beauty was his king.

John Drinkwater

335 From *The Builders*

Grant us the knowledge that we need
To solve the questions of the mind;
Light Thou our candles while we read,
To keep our hearts from going blind;
Enlarge our vision to behold
The wonders Thou hast wrought of old;
Reveal thyself in every law,
And gild the towers of truth with holy awe.

Henry van Dyke

336 *Omniscience*

Thou seest the under side of every leaf,
The arteries of earth are bare to Thee,
Before Thee hell is naked, every sea
Is crystal, every garnered sheaf,
Grain upon grain, Thou knowest; not a blade
Of withered grass the wind blows vagrantly
But at Thy nod; the nest-woof Thou dost see,
The speckling of the egg within is laid.

The wheeling planets Thou dost call by name,
There is no star so lost in utter space
Thou markest not its shining and its place,
And every hearth and every altar flame.
And souls of men are as a page outspread
Whereon Thou readest both of good and base:—
What falling rock shall hide us from Thy face?
May we escape Thy glance, though we be dead?

Yea, but Thou seest that our frame is weak,
  And that the thing we do is that we hate,
  Thou seest that we weep when it is late,
And wound the heart that loves us when we speak,
Thou knowest that our portion is but tears,
  We love to lose, are little and not great;—
  With Thy large glance Thou readest all our state,
And wilt be patient of our empty years.

Blanche Mary Kelly

337 *Petition*

Grant it, Father,
  That I live
Always in
  Superlative.

Eleanor Slater

3 · THE WORK OF OUR HANDS

338 ### From *Andrew Rykman's Prayer*

Make my mortal dreams come true
With the work I fain would do;
Clothe with life the weak intent,
Let me be the thing I meant;
Let me find in Thy employ
Peace that dearer is than joy;
Out of self to love be led
And to heaven acclimated,
Until all things sweet and good
Seem my natural habitude.

John Greenleaf Whittier

339 ### *Life-Mosaic*

Master, to do great work for Thee my hand
  Is far too weak. Thou givest what may suit—
  Some little chips to cut with care minute,
Or tint, or grave, or polish. Others stand
Before their quarried marble fair and grand,
  And make a life-work of the great design
  Which Thou hast traced; or, many-skilled, combine
To build vast temples, gloriously planned.
Yet take the tiny stones that I have wrought,
  Just one by one, as they were given by Thee,
Not knowing what came next in Thy wise thought;
Set each stone by Thy master-hand of grace,
  Form the mosaic as Thou wilt for me,
And in Thy temple-pavement give it place.

Frances Ridley Havergal

340

A Prayer

Let me work and be glad,
  O Lord, and I ask no more;
With will to turn where the sunbeams burn
  At the sill of my workshop door.

Aforetime I prayed my prayer
  For the glory and gain of earth,
But now grown wise and with opened eyes,
  I have seen what the prayer was worth.

Give me my work to do
  And peace of the task well done;
Youth of the Spring and its blossoming
  And the light of the moon and sun.

Pleasure of little things
  That never may pall or end,
And fast in my hold no lesser gold
  Than the honest hand of a friend.

Let me forget in time
  Folly of dreams that I had;
Give me my share of a world most fair—
  Let me work and be glad.

Theodosia Garrison

341

The Carpenter

O Lord, at Joseph's humble bench
  Thy hands did handle saw and plane;
Thy hammer nails did drive and clench,
  Avoiding knot and humouring grain.

⁂

Lord, might I be but as a saw,
  A plane, a chisel, in thy hand!—

No, Lord! I take it back in awe,
  Such prayer for me is far too grand.

I pray, O Master, let me lie,
  As on thy bench the favoured wood;
Thy saw, thy plane, thy chisel ply,
  And work me into something good.

No, no; ambition, holy-high,
  Urges for more than both to pray:
Come in, O gracious Force, I cry—
  O workman, share my shed of clay.

Then I, at bench, or desk, or oar,
  With knife or needle, voice or pen,
As thou in Nazareth of yore,
  Shall do the Father's will again.

Thus fashioning a workman rare,
  O Master, this shall be thy fee:
Home to thy father thou shalt bear
  Another child made like to thee.

George Macdonald

342 *O Son of Man, Thou Madest Known*

O Son of Man, Thou madest known,
Through quiet work in shop and home,
The sacredness of common things,
The chance of life that each day brings.

O Workman truc, may we fulfil
In daily life Thy Father's will;
In duty's call, Thy call we hear
To fuller life, thro' work sincere.

Thou Master Workman, grant us grace
The challenge of our tasks to face;

By loyal scorn of second best,
By effort true, to meet each test.

And thus we pray in deed and word,
Thy kingdom come on earth, O Lord.
In work that gives effect to prayer,
Thy purpose for Thy world we share.
Milton S. Littlefield

343 *The Artisan*

O God, my master God, look down and see
If I am making what Thou wouldst of me.
Fain might I lift my hands up in the air
From the defiant passion of my prayer:
Yet here they grope on this cold altar stone,
Graving the words I think I should make known.
Mine eyes are Thine. Yea, let me not forget,
Lest with unstaunchèd tears I leave them wet,
Dimming their faithful power, till they not see
Some small, plain task that might be done for Thee.
My feet, that ache for paths of flowery bloom,
Halt steadfast in the straitness of this room.
Though they may never be on errands sent,
Here shall they stay, and wait Thy full content.
And my poor heart, that does so crave for peace,
Shall beat until Thou bid its beating cease.
So, Thou dear master God, look down and see
Whether I do Thy bidding heedfully.
Alice Brown

344 *First Day of Teaching*

Now this is new: that I (habitué
Of classes where my thinking has been stirred
To surging tide or frothy ripple) stand
Before a class to speak instructive word.

I planned to have it so. Deliberately
I laid foundation for this moment. Yet . . .
I did not know my feet would feel so large . . .
O God of Teachers, may I not forget
Those neat assignments, practiced to the letter,
Those deftly fashioned phrases that I planned.
Now must I pass these papers. O dear God,
Let not the sheets go slithering from my hand.
And if You could but ring the fire alarm . . .
Or anything . . . O any sharp surprise
To turn away from my stiff dwindling self
These thirty pair of adolescent eyes.

Bonaro W. Overstreet

345 *Prayer of a Beginning Teacher*

Dear God, I humbly pray
  That Thou, with each passing day
  Wilt give me courage, wisdom true,
To meet each problem, see it thru—
  With wisdom and justice to teach each child
  To recognize the things worthwhile.
Help me to start them on the way
  To clean, brave living—day by day,
  So that tomorrow for each one
  Will be met squarely—and be won—
And as I help each little child
  To learn to love the things worthwhile,
  Lord, help me to be true;
  For I am just beginning, too.

Ouida Smith Dunnam

346 *Prayer of a Teacher*

Father, between Thy strong hands Thou has bent
The clay but roughly into shape, and lent

To me the task of smoothing where I may
And fashioning to a gentler form Thy clay.
To see some hidden beauty Thou hadst planned,
Slowly revealed beneath my laboring hand;
Sometimes to help a twisted thing to grow
More straight; this is full recompense, and so
I give Thee but the praise that Thou wouldst ask. . . .
Firm hand and high heart for the further task.

Dorothy Littlewort

347

The Teacher

Lord, who am I to teach the way
To little children day by day,
So prone myself to go astray?

I teach them knowledge, but I know
How faint they flicker and how low
The candles of my knowledge glow.

I teach them power to will and do,
But only now to learn anew
My own great weakness through and through.

I teach them love for all mankind
And all God's creatures, but I find
My love comes lagging far behind.

Lord, if their guide I still must be,
Oh, let the little children see
A teacher leaning hard on Thee.

Leslie Pinckney Hill

348

Prayer for the Pilot

Lord of Sea and Earth and Air,
Listen to the Pilot's prayer—

Send him wind that's steady and strong,
Grant that his engine sings the song
Of flawless tone, by which he knows
It shall not fail him where he goes;
Landing, gliding, in curve, half-roll—
Grant him, O Lord, a full control,
That he may learn in heights of Heaven
The rapture altitude has given,
That he shall know the joy they feel
Who ride Thy realms on Birds of Steel.

Cecil Roberts

349

Equipment

With what thou gavest me, O Master,
I have wrought.
Such chances, such abilities,
To see the end was not for my poor eyes,
Thine was the impulse, thine the forming thought.

Ah, I have wrought,
And these sad hands have right to tell their story,
It was no hard up striving after glory,
Catching and losing, gaining and failing,
Raging me back at the world's raucous railing.
Simply and humbly from stone and from wood,
Wrought I the things that to thee might seem good.

If they are little, ah God! but the cost,
Who but thou knowest the all that is lost!
If they are few, is the workmanship true?
Try them and weigh me, whate'er be my due!

Paul Laurence Dunbar

4 · THE DEDICATED LIFE

350 *Great God, I Ask Thee for No Meaner Pelf*

Great God, I ask thee for no meaner pelf
Than that I may not disappoint myself,
That in my action I may soar as high,
As I can now discern with this clear eye.

And next in value, which thy kindness lends,
That I may greatly disappoint my friends,
Howe'er they think or hope that it may be,
They may not dream how thou'st distinguished me.

That my weak hand may equal my firm faith,
And my life practice more than my tongue saith;
That my low conduct may not show,
Nor my relenting lines,
That I thy purpose did not know,
Or overrated thy designs.

Henry David Thoreau

351 *The Master's Touch*

In the still air the music lies unheard;
  In the rough marble beauty hides unseen;
To wake the music and the beauty, needs
  The master's touch, the sculptor's chisel keen.

Great Master, touch us with Thy skilful hand,
  Let not the music that is in us die;
Great Sculptor, hew and polish us; nor let,
  Hidden and lost, Thy form within us lie.

Spare not the stroke; do with us as Thou wilt;
  Let there be nought unfinished, broken, marred;
Complete Thy purpose, that we may become
  Thy perfect image, O our God and Lord.

Horatius Bonar

352 *The Celestial Surgeon*

If I have faltered more or less
In my great task of happiness;
If I have moved among my race
And shown no glorious morning face;
If beams from happy human eyes
Have moved me not; if morning skies,
Books, and my food, and summer rain
Knocked on my sullen heart in vain:—
Lord, thy most pointed pleasure take
And stab my spirit broad awake;
Or, Lord, if too obdurate I,
Choose thou, before that spirit die,
A piercing pain, a killing sin,
And to my dead heart run them in!

Robert Louis Stevenson

353 *The Passionate Sword*

Temper my spirit, O Lord,
  Burn out its alloy,
And make it a pliant steel for Thy wielding,
  Not a clumsy toy;
A blunt, iron thing in my hands
  That blunder and destroy.

Temper my spirit, O Lord,
  Keep it long in the fire;
Make it one with the flame. Let it share

That up-reaching desire.
Grasp it, Thyself, O my God;
Swing it straighter and higher!

Jean Starr Untermeyer

354 *Prayers of Steel*

Lay me on an anvil, O God.
Beat me and hammer me into a crowbar.
Let me pry loose old walls.
Let me lift and loosen old foundations.

Lay me on an anvil, O God.
Beat me and hammer me into a steel spike.
Drive me into the girders that hold a skyscraper together.
Take red-hot rivets and fasten me into the central girders.
Let me be the great nail holding a skyscraper through blue nights into white stars.

Carl Sandburg

355 *Worship*

Teach me the ritual that runs beyond
The rote of words, the flexing of the knee:
Let me be always, Lord of Life, with Thee!
In all my motions ready to respond
To Thy unveilings, though in Scripture conned.
Or in the mid-night's insect melody,
The scent of bloom from desert bush or tree,
The dawn's reflection in the blushing pond.

How shall I worship only for an hour?
How think Thee present under dome and spire
Or sense Thee in the wafer and the wine
Except the common bread and cup are Thine,
Thine shop and street, the hearth-stone and the fire,
Thine all the ministries of natural power?

Robert Whitaker

356 *Tune Me, O Lord, into One Harmony*

Tune me, O Lord, into one harmony
  With Thee, one full responsive vibrant chord;
Unto Thy praise, all love and melody,
  Tune me, O Lord.

Christina G. Rossetti

IX

PETITIONS OF DOUBT AND PROTEST

357 *Doubt*

O distant Christ, the crowded, darkening years
  Drift slow between thy gracious face and me:
  My hungry heart leans back to look for thee,
But finds the way set thick with doubts and fears.

My groping hands would touch thy garment's hem,
  Would find some token thou art walking near;
  Instead, they clasp but empty darkness drear,
And no diviner hands reach out to them.

Sometimes my listening soul, with bated breath,
  Stands still to catch a footfall by my side,
  Lest, haply, my earth-blinded eyes but hide
Thy stately figure, leading Life and Death;

My straining eyes, O Christ, but long to mark
  A shadow of thy presence, dim and sweet,
  Or far-off light to guide my wandering feet,
Or hope for hands prayer-beating 'gainst the dark.

O Thou! unseen by me, that like a child
  Tries in the night to find its mother's heart,
  And weeping wanders only more apart,
Not knowing in the darkness that she smiled—

Thou, all unseen, dost hear my tired cry,
  As I, in darkness of a half belief,
  Grope for thy heart, in love and doubt and grief:
O Lord! speak soon to me—"Lo, here am I!"

Margaret Deland

358 *The Doubter's Prayer*

Eternal Power, of earth and air!
  Unseen, yet seen in all around;

Remote, but dwelling everywhere;
  Though silent, heard in every sound;

If e'er Thine ear in mercy bent,
  When wretched mortals cried to Thee,
And if, indeed, Thy Son was sent,
  To save lost sinners such as me:

Then hear me now, while kneeling here,
  I lift to Thee my heart and eye,
And all my soul ascends in prayer,
  Oh, give me—give me faith! I cry.

Without some glimmering in my heart,
  I could not raise this fervent prayer;
But, oh! a stronger light impart,
  And in Thy mercy fix it there.

While Faith is with me, I am blest;
  It turns my darkest night to day;
But while I clasp it to my breast,
  I often feel it slide away.

Then, cold and dark, my spirit sinks,
  To see my light of life depart;
And every fiend of Hell, methinks,
  Enjoys the anguish of my heart.

What shall I do, if all my love,
  My hopes, my toil, are cast away,
And if there be no God above,
  To hear and bless me when I pray?

If this be vain delusion all,
  If death be an eternal sleep,
And none can hear my secret call,
  Or see the silent tears I weep!

Oh, help me, God! For Thou alone
  Canst my distracted soul relieve;
Forsake it not, it is Thine own,
  Though weak, yet longing to believe.

Oh, drive these cruel doubts away;
  And make me know that Thou art God!
A faith, that shines by night and day,
  Will lighten every earthly load.

If I believe that Jesus died,
  And waking, rose to reign above;
Then surely Sorrow, Sin, and Pride
  Must yield to Peace, and Hope, and Love;

And all the blessèd words He said
  Will strength and holy joy impart:
A shield of safety o'er my head,
  A spring of comfort in my heart.

Anne Brontë

359

Father

  Oh Father—if Thou wouldst indeed
Welcome Thy straying children home,
How eager were my heart to heed,
How humbly, gravely, would it come!

  I am no rude rebellious son
Contemptuous of Thy love's behest.
My broken fears would haste, would run
If Thou didst call me to Thy breast.

  Ah, in the midnight, in the dawn
I listened—and have never heard,
However faint or far-withdrawn,
The vibrance of Thy summoning word!

More harsh than jangled bolts and bars—
More cruel than promises forgone—
The senile silence of Thy stars,
The idiot radiance of Thy dawn.

Arthur Davison Ficke

360 *A Seeker in the Night*

I lift my eyes, but I cannot see;
I stretch my arms and I cry to Thee,—
And still the darkness covers me.

Where art Thou? In the chill obscure
I wander lonely, and endure
A yearning only Thou canst cure!

Once—once, indeed, in every face
I seemed thy lineaments to trace
And looked in all to find thy grace:

I thought the thrush—sweet worshipper!—
From the minaret of the balsam-fir
Hymned forth thy praise, my soul to stir;

I thought the early roses came
To lisp in fragrant breaths thy name,
And teach my heart to do the same;

I thought the stars thy candles, Lord!—
I thought the skylark as he soared
Rose to thy throne and Thee adored!

But now a labyrinth I wind,
And needing more thy hand to find,
Grope, darkling, Lord!—for I am blind!

Ah, bridge for me the awful vast,
That I may find Thee at the last!—
Then draw me close, and hold me fast!

Florence Earle Coates

361 *Prayer of an Unbeliever*

Draw closer to me, God, than were I one,
With the hedged comfort of a creed about,
With not a shadow's shadow of a doubt
That You are father, and each man a son.
Because I halt means not the will to roam,
But through the stubble a surer track to find:
Confused of foot, the ear, the eye less kind,
One fears to miss the steps which lead to home.
Who gives not to a wayfarer at the end
A roof? To beggar a sustaining cup?
Else waits the crumbling ditch from dew to dew.
Even this to me, if by that way I mend,
By such a bitter hand be lifted up,
To stumble to that lodging which is You.

Lizette Woodworth Reese

362 *The Doubter*

Thou Christ, my soul is hurt and bruised!
  With words the scholars wear me out;
My brain o'erwearied and confused,
  Thee, and myself, and all I doubt.

And must I back to darkness go
  Because I cannot say their creed?
I know not what I think; I know
  Only that thou art what I need.

Richard Watson Gilder

363 *Prayer for Living and Dying*

O dear and loving God,
So wide and broad
Thine altar it can hold as gift
My old agnosticism as the loving shift
In which is wrapped acceptance of my Lord.

Forgive me, then,
That all the mounting sharpness of my years
Has ripped the Sistine panoply of robes,
Scissored the beard Blake gave the Elohim,
Made large but never dim
Thyself as concept magnified by tears,
Globe within globe, the rhyme
With which immensity holds the space of time.

Allow me, as I thank for daily bread,
Christ but thy son as I am thus thy son:
Man's frailty overleaping human ways;
Thus marveling how thy miracle is done
Because I humbly praise
Mary's lost maidenhead.

I too the voice within the whirlwind heard,
Stood speechless, breathlessly,
Unknowing how to loose Orion's bands:
Knowing that thy unfingered hands
Cast loose the atom from inviolate chains
And with sweet word
Set up as borders to infinity
A universe without any yet within;
Hearing the voice, I beg to know all sin,
All evil till the good alone distrains.

And then, at last, O dear and loving God,
Blow on my ashes with thy welcoming breath,

Cover my doubts with the immortal sod,
Carve love deep on my death.

Christopher La Farge

364 *Bitter-Sweet*

Ah my deare angrie Lord,
Since thou dost love, yet strike;
Cast down, yet help afford;
Sure I will do the like.
I will complain, yet praise;
I will bewail, approve:
And all my sowre-sweet dayes
I will lament, and love.

George Herbert

365 *Scholfield Huxley*

God! ask me not to record your wonders,
I admit the stars and the suns
And the countless worlds.
But I have measured their distances
And weighed them and discovered their substances.
I have devised wings for the air,
And keels for water,
And horses of iron for the earth.
I have lengthened the vision you gave me a million times,
And the hearing you gave me a million times,
I have leaped over space with speech,
And taken fire for light out of the air.
I have built great cities and bored through the hills,
And bridged majestic waters.
I have written the Iliad and Hamlet;
And I have explored your mysteries,
And searched for you without ceasing,
And found you again after losing you
In hours of weariness—

And I ask you:
How would you like to create a sun
And the next day have the worms
Slipping in and out between your fingers?

Edgar Lee Masters

366

Supplication

For He knoweth our frame, He remembereth
that we are dust.—PSALM CIII. 14.

Oh Lord, when all our bones are thrust
Beyond the gaze of all but Thine;
And these blaspheming tongues are dust
Which babbled of Thy name divine,
How helpless then to carp or rail
Against the canons of Thy word;
Wilt Thou, when thus our spirits fail,
Have mercy, Lord?

Here from this ebon speck that floats
As but a mote within Thine eye,
Vain sneers and curses from our throats
Rise to the vault of Thy fair sky:
Yet when this world of ours is still
Of this all-wondering, tortured horde,
And none is left for Thou to kill—
Have mercy, Lord!

Thou knowest that our flesh is grass;
Ah! let our withered souls remain
Like stricken reeds of some morass,
Bleached, if Thou will, by ceaseless rain.
Have we not had enough of fire,
Enough of torment and the sword,
If these accrue from Thy desire?
Have mercy, Lord!

Dost Thou not see about our feet
The tangles of our erring thought?
Thou knowest that we run to greet
High hopes that vanish into naught.
We bleed, we fall, we rise again;
How can we be of Thee abhorred?
We are Thy breed, we little men—
Have mercy, Lord!

Wilt Thou then slay for that we slay,
Wilt Thou deny when we deny?
A thousand years are but a day,
A little day within Thine eye:
We thirst for love, we yearn for life;
We lust, wilt Thou the lust record?
We, beaten, fall upon the knife—
Have mercy, Lord!

Thou givest us youth that turns to age;
And strength that leaves us while we seek.
Thou pourest the fire of sacred rage
In costly vessels all too weak.
Great works we planned in hopes that Thou
Fit wisdom therefor wouldst accord;
Thou wrotest failure on our brow—
Have mercy, Lord!

Could we but know, as Thou dost know—
Hold the whole scheme at once in mind!
Yet, dost Thou watch our anxious woe
Who piece with palsied hands and blind
The fragments of our little plan,
To thrive and earn Thy blest reward,
And make and keep the world of man—
Have mercy, Lord!

Thou settest the sun within his place
  To light the world, the world is Thine,
Put in our hands and through Thy grace
  To be subdued and made divine.
Whether we serve Thee ill or well,
  Thou knowest our frame, nor canst afford
To leave Thy own for long in hell—
      Have mercy, Lord!

Edgar Lee Masters

367 *A Prayer in Late Autumn*

When Life has borne its harvest from my heart,
  And only tarnished husks are there,
Grotesquely stacked and bristling the worn ground,
  And there is winter in the air;
When, like this field, I wait, within my soul
  The scars of lost fertility,
And I am ugly, not with conquering strength,
  But with a sere fragility—
God, let me keep my sense of humor then;
  Grant me some clumsy power to shield
My awful dearth just as one pumpkin mocks,
  In clownish glee, this frosted field!

Violet Alleyn Storey

368 *If This Be All*

O God! if this indeed be all
  That Life can show to me;
If on my aching brow may fall
  No freshening dew from Thee;

If with no brighter light than this
  The lamp of hope may glow
And I may only *dream* of bliss,
  And wake to weary woe;

If friendship's solace must decay,
  When other joys are gone,
And love must keep so far away,
  While I go wandering on,—

Wandering and toiling without gain,
  The slave of others' will,
With constant care and frequent pain,
  Despised, forgotten still;

Grieving to look on vice and sin,
  Yet powerless to quell
The silent current from within,
  The outward torrent's swell;

While all the good I would impart,
  The feelings I would share,
Are driven backward to my heart,
  And turned to wormwood there;

If clouds must *ever* keep from sight
  The glories of the Sun,
And I must suffer Winter's blight,
  Ere Summer is begun:

If Life must be so full of care—
  Then call me soon to Thee;
Or give me strength enough to bear
  My load of misery.

Anne Brontë

369 *Prayer*

Let me not know how sins and sorrows glide
Along the sombre city of our rage,
Or why the sons of men are heavy-eyed.

Let me not know, except from printed page,
The pain of bitter love, of baffled pride,
Or sickness shadowing with a long presage.

Let me not know, since happy some have died
Quickly in youth or quietly in age,
How faint, how loud the bravest hearts have cried.

James Elroy Flecker

370 *Thou Art Indeed Just, Lord, If I Contend*

Thou art indeed just, Lord, if I contend
With thee; but, sir, so what I plead is just.
Why do sinners' ways prosper? and why must
Disappointment all I endeavour end?

Gerard Manley Hopkins

371 *Loneliness*

My soul has solitudes
Where no pace falls;
Thy silent trespassings
No man forestalls.

My soul has silences
No voice can break;
Only Thy hidden words
Its echoes wake.

But oh, the solitudes
Shouldst Thou not come!
The stricken silences,
When Thou art dumb!

Edwin Essex

X

THROUGH DEEP WATERS

1 · DE PROFUNDIS

372 *A Prayer*

Out of the deeps I cry to thee, O God!
I fain would bring my soul safe up the sky—
This shining jewel rainbowed like a tear,
This star in the body that belongs to heaven.
With all the straining strength of my poor might,
I stagger with it up the dreadful way—
O but I fear unless some succour comes,
Some kindness of some angel, or some help
From watching planet sad to see me climb,
That in some gulf the precious thing must fall.
For I am weak and weary, and all my will
Went in the miles behind me, and no more
Remains in me to face the frowning height.

Ah! is my soul, that is so much to me,
Nothing to thee, O God?
See in my hands that I stretch up to thee
The lovely thing thou gavest: let it not
Die ere I die—but rather pluck its light
Out of my brain, while still it brightly burns,
Not with my body gutters to decay.
Out of the deeps I cry to thee, O God!
I fain would bring my soul safe back to thee.

Richard Le Gallienne

373 *De Profundis*

Out of the utmost pitch of wilderment,
Out of the stunned distress of ignorance,
Amazement, laceration, and despair,

The offering trampled, the derided ardor spent,
  Deliver us, O Lord,
And make thy power our truth, our sight thy Word.

From consternation's stroke, and the last hope
Bereft, and darkness' shattering scimitar
Counselling madness, and the palsied stand
Of those who in the noontide totter and grope,
  Deliver us, O Lord,
Fed from thy secret manna's hidden hoard.

From the blanched visage of affright, the soul
Smit with the rod of horror, tasting so
Creation's *culs de sac* of death, and black
Relapses of the species from the destined goal,
  Deliver us, O Lord,
And set our souls the effulgent issue toward.

From dreadful death, the wasting and the fire,
Corruption, and the obscenity of decay,
The torture of mad thoughts, and conscious course
Of dissolution in sin's viewless pyre,
  Deliver us, O Lord,
With bread of health from life's abundant board.

Amos N. Wilder

374

To the Unknown Light

In the sad spirit
  Where all is dark
And fault and merit
  Are gray shapes stark,
Each like his neighbour
  And each dim,
And pleasure and labour
  Alike are grim,
Shine down, O Light,
Illumine this night.

Here in the gray
  Nor motion nor breath
Nor joy of day
  Nor sharpness of death
Relieves the endless
  Pitiless gloom
Where goeth friendless
  Desire to her doom:
Shine down, O Light,
Illumine this night.

I know thou livest,
  Then shine, then shine,
Thou that givest
  Help divine,
Turn on this cold
  Thy burning eyes
Ere starved and old
  The dark heart dies:
Shine down, O Light,
Illumine this night.

Edward Shanks

375 *A Better Resurrection*

I have no wit, no words, no tears;
  My heart within me like a stone
Is numbed too much for hopes or fears.
  Look right, look left, I dwell alone;
I lift mine eyes, but dimmed with grief
  No everlasting hills I see;
My life is in the falling leaf:
    O Jesus, quicken me.

My life is like a faded leaf,
  My harvest dwindled to a husk:
Truly my life is void and brief

And tedious in the barren dusk;
My life is like a frozen thing,
No bud nor greenness can I see;
Yet rise it shall—the sap of Spring;
O Jesus, rise in me.

My life is like a broken bowl,
A broken bowl that cannot hold
One drop of water for my soul
Or cordial in the searching cold;
Cast in the fire the perished thing;
Melt and remould it, till it be
A royal cup for Him, my King:
O Jesus, drink of me.

Christina G. Rossetti

376 *A Hymn to God in Time of Stress*

Lift, O dark and glorious Wonder,
Once again thy gleaming sword,
Cleave this killing doubt asunder
With one sheer and sacred word!

For my heart is weak and broken,
And the struggle runs too high,
And there is no burning token
In the new immortal sky.

Oh, not curb or courage only
Does my hour demand of me,
It is thought supreme and lonely
And responsible and free!

And I quail before the danger
As a bark before the blast,
When the beacon star's a stranger
In the mountains piling fast,

And there is no light but reason
And the compass of the ship.
God, a word of thine in season!
God, a motion of thy lip!

Max Eastman

377

In the Dark

Lord, since the strongest human hands I know
Reach through my darkness, will not let me go,
Hold me as if most dear when fallen most low;

Since, even now, when my spent courage lies
Stricken beneath disastrous, quivering skies,
I learn the tenderness of human eyes;

Surely, though night unthinkable impend,
Where human hands nor human eyes befriend,
Thou wilt avail me in the lonely end.

Sophie Jewett

378

Out of the Depths

Torn upon Thy wheel,
   Foul'd with blood and dust,
Still my heart can feel,
   Still trust;

Still my lips can urge,
   "Heal me with Thy sword,
Cleanse me with Thy scourge,
   Lord, Lord!"

Though a bleeding clod,
   Faint with thirst and pain,
Still my hopes, dear God,
   Remain;

Yea, and more than hope:
Faith! a prayer! a wing!
Even on Calvary's slope,
I sing!

Frederic Lawrence Knowles

379

A Psalm

O God, in whom my deepest being dwells,
Unasking what Thy form or mind may be,
Hear once again the sighing trust that wells
From my late wildered breast, and comfort me!
I call, I call from this long vale of tears,
I lift my eyes to the hills, there fancying Thee:
O Thou whose whim or wisdom shapes the spheres,
Yet be my temple and kind sanctuary!

The ages like an army without end
Go conquering on, and lay rich trophies by,
Their cities triumph and their fanes extend,
In their strong rooms the taken mysteries lie.
But thence does earth put on a lovelier hue?
Does their light hearten, or but terrify?
Fast cometh on my enemy anew,
And Bashan's arrows darken all the sky.

Thence as a bird, as that poor wood-pigeon,
Which with shot wings from the curst gunner flees
Through the wild scowling evening on and on
And finds a mercy in some secret trees,
I fly to Thee; I lodge me in those boughs
Which shadowed through the hottest tyrannies
Thy early shepherds; then refreshed I rouse,
Spring through white skies, and light in flowering leas.

Reason, still mining in her rocks and reefs,
Is still refining; fancy paints as Thee
A witenagemote of dæmon chiefs

For ever vying; forces not to see.
But nothing better than my fathers, I
Hear rather the heart's summons and go free
From all the heartless claims that multiply,
And still Thee Father call, and come to Thee.

Then though the light of the age far off reveal
Some tragic theme, and doubt grow doubly strong,
I happy am; I dare and need to kneel
To One who tuned great David's life to song.
My prayer, no more than not to lose that dew
And dawn that failed not yet my path along:
O God that Abraham and our Vaughan knew,
Hide not Thyself, let first love prove not wrong.

Edmund Blunden

380 From *De Profundis*

Whatever's lost, it first was won;
We will not struggle nor impugn.
Perhaps the cup was broken here,
That heaven's new wine might show more clear.
I praise Thee while my days go on.

I praise Thee while my days go on;
I love Thee while my days go on;
Through dark and dearth, through fire and frost,
With emptied arms and treasure lost,
I thank Thee while my days go on.

Elizabeth Barrett Browning

2 · THE CHASTENING OF PAIN

381 From *The Christian's New-Year Prayer*

If my vain soul needs blows and bitter losses
To shape it for Thy crown,
Then bruise it, burn it, burden it with crosses,
With sorrows bear it down.
Do what Thou wilt to mould me to Thy pleasure;
And if I should complain,
Heap full of anguish yet another measure
Until I smile at pain.
Send dangers—deaths! but tell me how to bear them;
Enfold me in Thy care.
Send trials—tears! but give me strength to bear them—
This is a Christian's prayer.

Ella Wheeler Wilcox

382 *Prayer for Pain*

I do not pray for peace nor ease,
Nor truce from sorrow:
No suppliant on servile knees
Begs here against to-morrow!

Lean flame against lean flame we flash
O Fates that meet me fair;
Blue steel against blue steel we clash—
Lay on, and I shall dare!

But Thou of deeps the awful Deep,
Thou breather in the clay,
Grant this my only prayer—O keep
My soul from turning gray!

For until now, whatever wrought
Against my sweet desires,
My days were smitten harps strung taut,
My nights were slumbrous lyres.

And howsoe'er the hard blow rang
Upon my battered shield,
Some lark-like, soaring spirit sang
Above my battle-field;

And through my soul of stormy night
The zigzag blue flame ran.
I asked no odds—I fought my fight—
Events against a man.

But now—at last—the gray mist chokes
And numbs me. Leave me pain!
O let me feel the biting strokes
That I may fight again!

John G. Neihardt

383 *A Prayer*

I pray not for the joy that knows
  No saving benison of tears;
The placid life of ease that flows
  Untroubled through the changing years.

Grant me, O God, the mind to see
  The blessings which my sorrows bring;
And give me, in adversity,
  The heart that still can trust and sing.

Marion Franklin Ham

384 *The Cup of Happiness*

Lord God, how full our cup of happiness!
We drink and drink—and yet it grows not less;

But every day the newly risen sun
Finds it replenished, sparkling, overrun.
Hast Thou not given us raiment, warmth, and meat,
And all the seasonable fruits to eat?—
Work for our hands, and rainbows for our eyes,
And for our minds the treasures of the wise?—
A father's smile, a mother's fond embrace,
The tender light upon a lover's face?—
The talk of friends, the twinkling eye of mirth,
The whispering silence of the good green earth?—
Hope for our youth, and memories for age,
And psalms upon the heavens' moving page?

And dost Thou not of pain a mingling pour,
To make the cup but overflow the more?

Gilbert Thomas

385 *Prayer under the Pressure of Violent Anguish*[1]

I

O Thou Great Being! what Thou art
  Surpasses me to know;
Yet sure I am, that known to Thee
  Are all Thy works below.

II

Thy creature here before Thee stands,
  All wretched and distrest;
Yet sure those ills that wring my soul
  Obey Thy high behest.

III

Sure Thou, Almighty, canst not act
  From cruelty or wrath!
O, free my weary eyes from tears,
  Or close them fast in death!

[1] There was a certain period of life that my spirit was broke by repeated losses and disasters. In this wretched state I hung my harp on the willow-trees except in some lucid intervals, in one of which I composed the following. R. B.

IV

But, if I must afflicted be
  To suit some wise design,
Then man my soul with firm resolves
  To bear and not repine!

Robert Burns

386

Security

Outwit me, Lord, if ever hence
  This unremembering brain
Should urge these most inconstant feet
  To quit Thy side again.

Be not too sure of me though death
  Still find me at Thy side,—
Let Pain, Thy soldier, break my legs
  Before I shall have died.

And when at length this heart is stopped,
  Leave not a final chance,
But send some kind centurion,
  An expert with the lance.

Charles L. O'Donnell

387

Process

The seed, Lord, falls on stony ground
  Which sun and rain can never bless—
Until the soil is broken found—
  With harvest fruitfulness.

Plow then the rock, and plow again,
  That so some blade of good may start,

After the searching share of pain
Has cut a furrow through my heart.
Charles L. O'Donnell

388 *A Prayer in Time of Blindness*

There are blind eyes
Who cannot see the glory of proud stars
Laughing in golden torrents
Across the dusty sky. . . .
Who cannot see the sunned ripples of lakes,
Nor the green fire of June,
Nor the wild frozen joy
Of snow-still fields.

May I always have eyes to see
The heartdrops of dew in a drooping pansy
In the drowsy dawn,
And the thin magnificence of beating gnat-wings
Curvetting through the perilous alley-air
In the pale dusk.

There are blind hearts
Who cannot throb to the black woe
Of a sweet land desolate
With bodies creaking at a rope's end. . . .
Who cannot ache with milk-starved babies,
Nor flame in crimson wrath
At justice scourged and racked and tortured,
At greed splitting brother from brother.

May my heart never grow deaf
To the whisper of suffering:
And my arm bruise to feebleness,
Eyes dim, and heart burn cindery,
Trudging the hard gay road
Of the clean-souled sons of men.
Clement Wood

389 *Be Thou My Guide*

Be Thou my guide, and I will walk in darkness
As one who treads the beamy heights of day,
Feeling a gladness amid desert sadness,
And breathing vernal fragrance all the way.

Be Thou my wealth, and, reft of all besides Thee,
I will forget the strife for meaner things,
Blest in the sweetness of thy rare completeness,
And opulent beyond the dream of kings.

Be Thou my strength, O lowly One and saintly!
And, though unvisioned ills about me throng,
Though danger woo me and deceit pursue me,
Yet in the thought of Thee I will be strong!

Florence Earle Coates

390 *Prayer in Affliction*

Keep me from bitterness. It is so easy
To nurse sharp, bitter thoughts each dull, dark hour!
Against self-pity, Man of Sorrows, defend me
With Thy deep sweetness and Thy gentle power!
And out of all this hurt of pain and heartbreak
Help me to harvest a new sympathy
For suffering humankind, a wiser pity
For those who lift a heavier cross with Thee!

Violet Alleyn Storey

391 From *A Dream of Artemis*

God, whose kindly hand doth sow
The rainbow showers on hill and lawn,
To make the young sweet grasses grow
And fill the udder of the fawn;
Whose light is life of leaf and flower,

And all the colours of the birds;
Whose song goes on from hour to hour
Upon the river's liquid words;
Reach to a golden beam of thine
And touch her pain. Your finger tips
Do make the violets' blue eclipse
Like milk upon a daisy shine.

God, who lights the little stars,
And over night the white dew spills;
Whose hand doth move the season's cars
And clouds that mock our pointed hills;
Whose bounty fills the cow-trod wold,
And fills with bread the warm brown sod;
Who brings us sleep, where we grow old
'Til sleep and age together nod;

Reach out a beam and touch the pain
A heart has oozed thro' all the years.
Your pity dries the morning's tears
And fills the world with joy again!

Francis Ledwidge

392 *Hymne to God My God, in My Sicknesse*[1]

Since I am coming to that Holy roome,
  Where, with thy Quire of Saints for evermore,
I shall be made thy Musique; As I come
  I tune the Instrument here at the dore,
  And what I must doe then, thinke here before.

❉

We thinke that Paradise and Calvarie,
  Christs Crosse, and Adams tree, stood in one place;
Looke, Lord, and finde both Adams met in me;
  As the first Adams sweat surrounds my face,
  May the last Adams blood my soule embrace.

[1] Written eight days before the poet's death.

So, in his purple wrapp'd receive mee Lord,
By these his thornes give me his other Crowne;
And as to others soules I preach'd thy word,
Be this my Text, my Sermon to mine owne,
Therefore that he may raise the Lord throws down.

John Donne

393 *Variations on a Theme by George Herbert*

After so many deaths to breathe again,
To see the clouded windows open, brighten
With recovered sight. To see the blackness whiten
And fountained love gush from the arid plain.

"*After so many deaths to live and write*"
Thou subtle God of Visions who has led
My footsteps to this room, this hour, this night
That I might testify my resurrection.

Now song pours from a thousand instruments
And my new-opened eyes drink in the sound,
The seeing ear, the thinking, speaking heart,
Refreshed again after long banishments.

Praise for the dark that taught me love of light!
Praise for the ill that made me long for health,
Praise for the death that taught me all life is,
I praise the mortal wound that made me His!

Marya Zaturenska

394 *A Prayer after Illness*

Tune me for life again, oh, quiet Musician.
Strive to adjust my loosened thoughts until,
Made taut, they shall be yielding to Thy Fingers
Gladly as trees to wind that touch this hill.

Rhyme me with life once more, oh, silent Poet.
  Out of my weary, fluttering heartbeats make
Cool rhythms, hushed, yet certain as the circling
  Water against the edges of this lake.

Fit me for life again, oh, patient Artist.
  Paint on my tired soul glad, vivid things.
Splash now, upon its dulness, beauty's pigments,
  Lovely as pansies or a bluebird's wings!

Violet Alleyn Storey

395 *Sonnet*

An open wound which has been healed anew;
A stream dried up, that once again is fed
With waters making green its grassy bed;
A tree that withered was, but to the dew
Puts forth young leaves and blossoms fresh of hue
Even from the branches which had seemed most dead;
A sea which having been disquieted,
Now stretches like a mirror calm and blue,—
Our hearts to each of these were likened well.
But Thou wert the physician and the balm;
Thou, Lord, the fountain, whence anew was filled
Their parchéd channel; Thou the dew that fell
On their dead branches; 'twas thy voice that stilled
The storm within; Thou didst command the calm.

Richard Chenevix Trench

396 *If This Were Faith*

God, if this were enough,
That I see things bare to the buff
And up to the buttocks in mire;
That I ask nor hope nor hire,
Nut in the husk,

Nor dawn beyond the dusk,
Nor life beyond death:
God, if this were faith?

Having felt thy wind in my face
Spit sorrow and disgrace,
Having seen thine evil doom
In Golgotha and Khartoum,
And the brutes, the work of thine hands,
Fill with injustice lands
And stain with blood the sea:
If still in my veins the glee
Of the black night and the sun
And the lost battle, run:
If, an adept,
The iniquitous lists I still accept
With joy, and joy to endure and be withstood,
And still to battle and perish for a dream of good:
God, if that were enough?

If to feel, in the ink of the slough,
And the sink of the mire,
Veins of glory and fire
Run through and transpierce and transpire,
And a secret purpose of glory in every part,
And the answering glory of battle fill my heart;
To thrill with the joy of girded men
To go on for ever and fail and go on again,
And be mauled to the earth and arise,
And contend for the shade of a word and a thing not seen with
the eyes:
With the half of a broken hope for a pillow at night
That somehow the right is the right
And the smooth shall bloom from the rough:
Lord, if that were enough?

Robert Louis Stevenson

397 *Ode*

How are thy servants blest, O Lord!
How sure is their defence!
Eternal wisdom is their guide,
Their help Omnipotence.

In foreign realms, and lands remote,
Supported by thy care,
Thro' burning climes I pass'd unhurt,
And breath'd in tainted air.

Thy mercy sweetned ev'ry soil,
Made ev'ry region please;
And hoary Alpine hills it warm'd,
And smooth'd the Tyrrhene seas.

Think, O my Soul, devoutly think,
How with affrighted eyes
Thou saw'st the wide extended deep
In all its horrors rise!

Confusion dwelt in ev'ry face,
And fear in ev'ry heart;
When waves on waves, and gulphs in gulphs,
O'ercame the pilot's art.

Yet then from all my griefs, O Lord,
Thy Mercy set me free,
Whilst in the confidence of pray'r
My soul took hold on thee;

For tho' in dreadful whirles we hung
High on the broken wave,
I knew thou wert not slow to hear,
Nor impotent to save.

The storm was laid, the winds retir'd,
  Obedient to thy will;
The sea that roar'd at thy command,
  At thy command was still.

In midst of dangers, fears and death,
  Thy goodness I'll adore,
And praise thee for thy mercies past;
  And humbly hope for more.

My life, if Thou preserv'st my life,
  Thy sacrifice shall be;
And death, if death must be my doom,
  Shall join my soul to thee.

Joseph Addison

398

A Prayer

O for one minute hark what we are saying!
  This is not pleasure that we ask of Thee!
Nay, let all life be weary of our praying,
  Streaming of tears and bending of the knee:—

Only we ask thro' shadows of the valley
  Stay of thy staff and guiding of thy rod,
Only, when rulers of the darkness rally,
  Be thou beside us, very near, O God!

Frederic W. H. Myers

XI
TOWARD THE LARGER LIFE

1 · WHEN THE SHADOWS LENGTHEN

399 *Let Me Grow Lovely*

Let me grow lovely, growing old—
So many fine things do:
Laces, and ivory, and gold,
And silks need not be new;

And there is healing in old trees,
Old streets a glamour hold:
Why may not I, as well as these,
Grow lovely, growing old?

Karle Wilson Baker

400 *Prayer*

Lord God of the oak and the elm,
And of the gray-green fields,
And the silver skies;
Lord God of the birds and the clouds,
And the rustling of leaves—

Ah, Green Bough in my heart burgeoning, blossoming,
All the days of my youth have been spent in the courts of thy praise!

I have loved Thee, worshiped Thee, adored Thee;
I have uncovered my heart where Thou liest hid,
That men might behold thine infinite healing and mercy;
Thou hast been my Refuge and Strength.
Be with me still,
When my life creeps into the shadows;
When Age has consumed my Endeavor,
And Ardor has flown;

When the hills are dreamy with April,
And I scarce can see them for dimness;
When the children laugh and call in the lane,
And I cannot go out to them. . .
Be with me still;
Shake down thy dusky dew over the fading landscape of my day;
And when the darkness comes,
Set Thou thy stars and constellations
In the heavens of my peace,
That still, through the watches of the night,
I may behold Thee, worship Thee, adore Thee—
And in the Great Dawn
Be made one with Thee,
O Lord my God, my Lover, and my Friend.

George Villiers

401

Weary in Well-Doing

I would have gone; God bade me stay:
  I would have worked; God bade me rest.
He broke my will from day to day;
  He read my yearnings unexprest,
    And said them nay.

Now I would stay; God bids me go:
  Now I would rest; God bids me work.
He breaks my heart tost to and fro;
  My soul is wrung with doubts that lurk
    And vex it so.

I go, Lord, where Thou sendest me;
  Day after day I plod and moil;
But, Christ my God, when will it be
  That I may let alone my toil
    And rest with Thee?

Christina G. Rossetti

402 From *Prayer of Columbus*

Thou knowest my years entire, my life,
My long and crowded life of active work, not adoration merely;
Thou knowest the prayers and vigils of my youth,
Thou knowest my manhood's solemn and visionary meditations,
Thou knowest I have in age ratified all those vows and strictly
    kept them,
Thou knowest I have not once lost nor faith nor ecstasy in Thee,
In shackles, prison'd, in disgrace, repining not,
Accepting all from Thee, as duly come from Thee.

All my emprises have been fill'd with Thee,
My speculations, plans, begun and carried on in thought of Thee,
Sailing the deep or journeying the land for Thee;
Intentions, purports, aspirations mine, leaving results to Thee.

❈

One effort more, my altar this bleak sand;
That Thou O God my life hast lighted,
With ray of light, steady, ineffable, vouchsafed of Thee,
Light rare untellable, lighting the very light,
Beyond all signs, descriptions, languages;
For that O God, be it my latest word, here on my knees,
Old, poor, and paralyzed, I thank Thee.

My terminus near,
The clouds already closing in upon me,
The voyage balk'd, the course disputed, lost,
I yield my ships to Thee.

My hands, my limbs grow nerveless,
My brain feels rack'd, bewilder'd,
Let the old timbers part, I will not part,
I will cling fast to Thee, O God, though the waves buffet me,
Thee, Thee at least I know.

Walt Whitman

403 *A Litany for Old Age*

When stealthy age creeps on me unaware
And, undetected, robs me of my powers,
When I must learn to face infirmity,
Then from rebellion, Lord,
Deliver me.

When all that is familiar fades away
And I must tread a new, uncertain path
Finding no landmarks save in memory,
Oh then from sick self-pity, Lord,
Deliver me.

And when the tide of life begins to ebb
And neither grief nor joy can stir my soul,
When time begins to merge into eternity,
Then from the craven fear of death
Good Lord, deliver me.

Una W. Harsen

404 *Uselessness*

Let mine not be the saddest fate of all
To live beyond my greater self; to see
My faculties decaying, as the tree
Stands stark and helpless while its green leaves fall.
Let me hear rather the imperious call,
Which all men dread, in my glad morning time,
And follow death ere I have reached my prime,
Or drunk the strengthening cordial of life's gall.
The lightning's stroke or the fierce tempest blast
Which fells the green tree to the earth to-day
Is kindlier than the calm that lets it last,
Unhappy witness of its own decay.
May no man ever look on me and say,
"She lives, but all her usefulness is past."

Ella Wheeler Wilcox

2 · LAST LINES

405 *Dust to Dust*

Heavenly Archer, bend thy bow;
Now the flame of life burns low,
Youth is gone; I, too, would go.

Even Fortune leads to this:
Harsh or kind, at last she is
Murderess of all ecstasies.

Yet the spirit, dark, alone,
Bound in sense, still hearkens on
For tidings of a bliss foregone.

Sleep is well for dreamless head,
At no breath astonishèd,
From the Gardens of the Dead.

I the immortal harps hear ring,
By Babylon's river languishing.
Heavenly Archer, loose thy string.

Walter de la Mare

406 *They Toil Not Neither Do They Spin*

Clother of the lily, Feeder of the sparrow,
 Father of the fatherless, dear Lord,
Tho' Thou set me as a mark against Thine arrow,
 As a prey unto Thy sword,
As a ploughed-up field beneath Thy harrow,
 As a captive in Thy cord,
Let that cord be love; and some day make my narrow
 Hallowed bed according to Thy Word. Amen.

Christina G. Rossetti

407

For My Funeral

O thou that from thy mansion
Through time and place to roam,
Dost send abroad thy children,
And then dost call them home,

That men and tribes and nations
And all thy hand hath made
May shelter them from sunshine
In thine eternal shade:

We now to peace and darkness
And earth and thee restore
Thy creature that thou madest
And wilt cast forth no more.

A. E. Housman

408

Valley of the Shadow

God, I am travelling out to death's sea,
I, who exulted in sunshine and laughter,
Thought not of dying—death is such waste of me!—
Grant me one prayer: Doom not the hereafter
Of mankind to war, as though I had died not—
I, who in battle, my comrade's arm linking,
Shouted and sang—life in my pulses hot
Throbbing and dancing! Let not my sinking
In dark be for naught, my death a vain thing!
God, let me know it the end of man's fever!
Make my last breath a bugle call, carrying
Peace o'er the valleys and cold hills for ever!

John Galsworthy

409

At Last

When on my day of life the night is falling,
And, in the winds from unsunned spaces blown,

I hear far voices out of darkness calling
  My feet to paths unknown,

Thou who hast made my home of life so pleasant,
  Leave not its tenant when its walls decay;
O Love Divine, O Helper ever present,
  Be Thou my strength and stay!

Be near me when all else is from me drifting;
  Earth, sky, home's pictures, days of shade and shine,
And kindly faces to my own uplifting
  The love which answers mine.

I have but Thee, my Father! let Thy spirit
  Be with me then to comfort and uphold;
No gate of pearl, no branch of palm I merit,
  Nor street of shining gold.

Suffice it if—my good and ill unreckoned,
  And both forgiven through Thy abounding grace—
I find myself by hands familiar beckoned
  Unto my fitting place.

Some humble door among Thy many mansions,
  Some sheltering shade where sin and striving cease,
And flows forever through heaven's green expansions
  The river of Thy peace.

There, from the music round about me stealing,
  I fain would learn the new and holy song,
And find at last, beneath Thy trees of healing,
  The life for which I long.

John Greenleaf Whittier

410 *Let Me Not Die*

Let me not die till death is due to come,
Lord, I care not if it be soon or late,
Only let no corrupt preludium

Of shadow wash me in its fetid spate.
Loose thou the fruit while it is round and lush,
Pick it or let it drop against the grass
Before the sagging pulp turns winey mush,
Or frost constricts the rind to ebon glass.
Blot out my sun one minute beyond noon;
Let it not droop upon the downward curve.
Lord, I care not if it be late or soon,
Only let not my soul, tangential, swerve
Upon that sin, which, growing infinite,
Sweeps down and down and down into the pit.

Edith Lovejoy Pierce

411 *Last Plea*

Oh, God, let me be beautiful in death,
Lend me, one moment in Eternity, Your making hand.
Oh, let the leaping spirals of my breath
Droop over me and hide
My bitten heart, my scarrèd side;
Let me walk proud and lovely from the land.

Have I misread the Law? Then give me sight.
Spare me, this awful once, the fumbling pattern of the blind.
Untether my impatience. In the night
Lean down in secret and retrace
Your symmetry upon my face;
Ballast by Your bright strength my failing might.

Jean Starr Untermeyer

412 From *Death*

Bid me remember, O my gracious Lord,
The flattering words of love are merely breath!
O not in roses wreathe the shining sword,
Bid me remember, O my gracious Lord,
The bitter taste of death!

Wrap not in clouds of dread for me that hour
When I must leave behind this house of clay,
When the grass withers and the shrunken flower!
Bid me, O Lord, in that most dreadful hour,
Not fall, but fly away!

Mary Elizabeth Coleridge

413 From *Last Lines*

Lord! if in love, though fainting oft, I have tended thy gracious Vine,
O, quench the thirst on these dying lips, Thou who pourest the wine!

Owen Meredith

414 *For Sleep, or Death*

Cure me with quietness,
Bless me with peace;
Comfort my heaviness,
Stay me with ease.
Stillness in solitude
Send down like dew;
Mine armour of fortitude
Pierce and make new:
That when I rise again
I may shine bright
As the sky after rain,
Day after night.

Ruth Pitter

415 *Let Me Go Down to Dust*

Let me go down to dust and dreams
Gently, O Lord, with never a fear
Of death beyond the day that is done;
In such a manner as beseems
A kinsman of the wild, a son

Of stoic earth whose race is run.
Let me go down as any deer,
Who, broken by a desperate flight,
Sinks down to slumber for the night—
Dumbly serene in certitude
That it will rise again at dawn,
Buoyant, refreshed of limb, renewed,
And confident that it will thrill
Tomorrow to its nuzzling fawn,
To the bugle-notes of elk upon the hill.

Let me go down to dreams and dust
Gently, O Lord, with quiet trust
And the fortitude that marks a child
Of earth, a kinsman of the wild.
Let me go down as any doe
That nods upon its ferny bed,
And, lulled to slumber by the flow
Of talking water, the muffled brawl
Of far cascading waterfall,
At last lets down its weary head
Deep in the brookmints in the glen;
And under the starry-candled sky,
With never the shadow of a sigh,
Gives its worn body back to earth again.

Lew Sarett

416 *D'Avalos' Prayer*

When the last sea is sailed, when the last shallow's charted,
When the last field is reaped, and the last harvest stored,
When the last fire is out and the last guest departed,
Grant the last prayer that I shall pray, be good to me, O Lord.

And let me pass in a night at sea, a night of storm and thunder,
In the loud crying of the wind through sail and rope and spar,
Send me a ninth great peaceful wave to drown and roll me under
To the cold tunny-fish's home where the drowned galleons are.

And in the dim green quiet place far out of sight and hearing,
Grant I may hear at whiles the wash and thresh of the sea-foam
About the fine keen bows of the stately clippers steering
Towards the lone northern star and the fair ports of home.

John Masefield

417 *The Last Invocation*

At the last, tenderly,
From the walls of the powerful fortress'd house,
From the clasp of the knitted locks, from the keep of the well-closed
  doors,
Let me be wafted.

Let me glide noiselessly forth;
With the key of softness unlock the locks—with a whisper,
Set ope the doors O soul.

Tenderly—be not impatient,
(Strong is your hold O mortal flesh,
Strong is your hold O love.)

Walt Whitman

418 *A Prayer in the Prospect of Death*

O Thou unknown, Almighty Cause
  Of all my hope and fear!
In whose dread presence, ere an hour,
  Perhaps I must appear!

If I have wander'd in those paths
  Of life I ought to shun—
As something, loudly, in my breast,
  Remonstrates I have done—

Thou know'st that Thou hast formèd me
  With passions wild and strong;

And list'ning to their witching voice
Has often led me wrong.

Where human weakness has come short,
Or frailty stept aside,
Do Thou, All-good—for such Thou art—
In shades of darkness hide.

Where with intention I have err'd,
No other plea I have,
But, Thou art good; and Goodness still
Delighteth to forgive.

Robert Burns

419 *No Coward Soul Is Mine*

No coward soul is mine,
No trembler in the world's storm-troubled sphere!
I see Heaven's glories shine,
And Faith shines equal, arming me from Fear.

O God within my breast,
Almighty ever-present Deity!
Life, that in me hast rest
As I, undying Life, have power in thee!

Vain are the thousand creeds
That move men's hearts, unutterably vain;
Worthless as withered weeds,
Or idlest froth, amid the boundless main

To waken doubt in one
Holding so fast by thy infinity,
So surely anchored on
The steadfast rock of immortality.

With wide-embracing love
Thy spirit animates eternal years,

Pervades and broods above,
Changes, sustains, dissolves, creates and rears.

Though earth and moon were gone,
And suns and universes ceased to be,
And thou wert left alone,
Every Existence would exist in thee.

There is not room for Death,
Nor atom that his might could render void
Since thou art Being and Breath,
And what thou art may never be destroyed.

Emily Brontë

420 *Closing Prayer*

Lord, lay your fingers on
My frightened eyes,
And hold your hand against
My heaving heart.

Prepare me for the shock
Of sweet surprise—
That moment when my soul
And body part!

Johnstone G. Patrick

421 *The Gardener*

O Love, when in my day of doom
The stone of sense from off me rolls,
Then from this earth, a barren tomb,
Do Thou, the Gardener of souls,
Uproot and bear me in Thy Breast,
And plant me where it please Thee best!

Laurence Housman

422 From *In Memoriam, A. C. M. L.*

God of all power and might,
Giver of all good things,
Who foldest day and night
In Thy almighty wings:
Thou who didst draw the plan,
And light the lamp of the sun,
And kindle the soul of man;
Now that the task is done,
Grant to me, crown of it all,
Grant me the final grace:
Master, hear my call;
Master, show Thy face.

Cecil Arthur Spring-Rice

3 · BEYOND DEATH

423 *What Am I Who Dare*

What am I who dare call thee God!
And raise my fancie to discourse thy power?
To whom dust is the period,
Who am not sure to farme this very houre?
For how know I the latest sand
In my fraile glasse of life, doth not now fall?
And while I thus astonisht stand
I but prepare for my owne funerall?
Death doth with man no order keepe:
It reckons not by the expence of yeares.
But makes the Queene and beggar weepe,
And nere distinguishes betweene their teares.
He who the victory doth gaine
Falls as he him pursues, who from him flyes,
And is by too good fortune slaine.
The Lover in his amorous courtship dyes.
The states-man suddenly expires
While he for others ruine doth prepare:
And the gay Lady while sh' admires
Her pride, and curles in wanton nets her haire.
No state of man is fortified
'Gainst the assault of th' universall doome:
But who th' Almightie feare, deride
Pale death, and meete with triumph in the tombe.

William Habington

424 From *In Memoriam A. H. H.*

Strong Son of God, immortal Love,
Whom we, that have not seen thy face,

By faith, and faith alone, embrace,
Believing where we cannot prove;

Thine are these orbs of light and shade;
Thou madest Life in man and brute;
Thou madest Death; and lo, thy foot
Is on the skull which thou hast made.

Thou wilt not leave us in the dust:
Thou madest man, he knows not why,
He thinks he was not made to die;
And thou hast made him: thou art just.

Thou seemest human and divine,
The highest, holiest manhood, thou.
Our wills are ours, we know not how;
Our wills are ours, to make them thine.

Our little systems have their day;
They have their day and cease to be;
They are but broken lights of thee,
And thou, O Lord, art more than they.

We have but faith: we cannot know,
For knowledge is of things we see;
And yet we trust it comes from thee,
A beam in darkness: let it grow.

Let knowledge grow from more to more,
But more of reverence in us dwell;
That mind and soul, according well,
May make one music as before,

But vaster. We are fools and slight;
We mock thee when we do not fear:
But help thy foolish ones to bear;
Help thy vain worlds to bear thy light.

Forgive what seem'd my sin in me,
  What seem'd my worth since I began;
  For merit lives from man to man,
And not from man, O Lord, to thee.

Forgive my grief for one removed,
  Thy creature, whom I found so fair.
  I trust he lives in thee, and there
I find him worthier to be loved.

Forgive these wild and wandering cries,
  Confusions of a wasted youth;
  Forgive them where they fail in truth,
And in thy wisdom make me wise.

Alfred Tennyson

425 From *A Poem*

Father of all! in Death's relentless claim
We read thy mercy by its sterner name;
In the bright flower that decks the solemn bier,
We see thy glory in its narrowed sphere;
In the deep lessons that affliction draws,
We trace the curves of thy encircling laws;
In the long sigh that sets our spirits free,
We own the love that calls us back to Thee!

Oliver Wendell Holmes

426 *Oh, Thou! Who Dry'st the Mourner's Tear*

Oh, Thou! who dry'st the mourner's tear,
  How dark this world would be,
If, when deceiv'd and wounded here,
  We could not fly to Thee!
The friends, who in our sunshine live,
  When winter comes, are flown;
And he who has but tears to give,

Must weep those tears alone.
But thou wilt heal that broken heart,
Which, like the plants that throw
Their fragrance from the wounded part,
Breathes sweetness out of woe.

When joy no longer soothes or cheers,
And even the hope that threw
A moment's sparkle o'er our tears,
Is dimm'd and vanish'd too,
Oh, who would bear life's stormy doom,
Did not thy Wing of Love
Come, brightly wafting through the gloom
Our Peace-branch from above?
Then sorrow, touch'd by Thee, grows bright
With more than rapture's ray;
As darkness shows us worlds of light
We never saw by day!

Thomas Moore

427 *In the Time of Trouble*

How hard for unaccustomed feet
Which only knew the meadow
Is this bleak road they now must tread
Through valleys dark with shadow.
Until they learn how sure Thy love
That girds each day, each morrow,
O Father, gently lead all hearts
That newly come to sorrow!

Leslie Savage Clark

428 *Missing*

Thou that didst leave the ninety and the nine
To seek the one,
Behold, among the many that are mine,
A lamb is gone.

The one perchance the worthiest to be,
  Dear Lord, with Thee;
And so the saddest for the Mother's heart
  With him to part.

O Thou, Thyself a mourning Mother's Son,
  Fold close my little one!

John Banister Tabb

429

Vesta

O Christ of God! whose life and death
  Our own have reconciled,
Most quietly, most tenderly
  Take home Thy star-named child!

Thy grace is in her patient eyes,
  Thy words are on her tongue;
The very silence round her seems
  As if the angels sung.

Her smile is as a listening child's
  Who hears its mother call;
The lilies of Thy perfect peace
  About her pillow fall.

She leans from out our clinging arms
  To rest herself in Thine;
Alone to Thee, dear Lord, can we
  Our well-beloved resign.

Oh, less for her than for ourselves
  We bow our heads and pray;
Her setting star, like Bethlehem's,
  To Thee shall point the way!

John Greenleaf Whittier

430 *A Prayer for the New Year*

God, patient of beginnings,
Help us this day to see
Time has no real beginning, no real end,
Just continuity.

'Though we are glibly saying,
In one excited breath,
"The Old Year dies; the New Year lives!" O, God,
Teach us Time knows no death!

Bid us consider gardens;
Seeds planted in the May,
Then flowers, then frost, then rest, and flowers once more.
And Time yields life this way!

Show us now cause for trusting,
Who would be fearful when
Years go and come, for life Time bears away,
Time will bring back again.

Teach us that years, in passing,
Heal, pardon, make us wise.
Teach us that days, in coming, bring with them
Fulfillment and surprise.

God, patient of beginnings,
Help us this day to see
In earthly bulbs, spring flowers; in man, the Christ;
In years, eternity!

Violet Alleyn Storey

431 *Prayer to the Father in Heaven*

O Radiant Luminary of light interminable,
Celestial Father, potential God of might,

Of heaven and earth O Lord incomparable,
  Of all perfections the Essential most perfite!
  O Maker of mankind, that formèd day and night,
Whose power imperial comprehendeth every place!
  Mine heart, my mind, my thought, my whole delight
Is, after this life, to see thy glorious Face.

Whose magnificence is incomprehensible,
  All arguments of reason which far doth exceed,
Whose Deity doubtless is indivisible,
  From whom all goodness and virtue doth proceed,
  Of thy support all creatures have need:
Assist me, good Lord, and grant me of thy grace
  To live to thy pleasure in word, thought, and deed,
And, after this life, to see thy glorious Face.

John Skelton

432 ## *After-Song*

Through love to light! O, wonderful the way
That leads from darkness to the perfect day!
From darkness and from sorrow of the night
To morning that comes singing o'er the sea.
Through love to light! Through light, O God, to Thee,
Who art the love of love, the eternal light of light!

Richard Watson Gilder

433 ## *When I Awake I Am Still with Thee*

Still, still with Thee, when purple morning breaketh,
  When the bird waketh and the shadows flee;
Fairer than morning, lovelier than the daylight,
  Dawns the sweet consciousness, *I am with Thee!*

Alone with Thee, amid the mystic shadows,
  The solemn hush of nature newly born;
Alone with Thee in breathless adoration,
  In the calm dew and freshness of the morn.

As in the dawning o'er the waveless ocean
  The image of the morning star doth rest,
So in this stillness Thou beholdest only
  Thine image in the waters of my breast.

Still, still with Thee! as to each new-born morning
  A fresh and solemn splendor still is given,
So doth this blessed consciousness, awaking,
  Breathe, each day, nearness unto Thee and heaven.

When sinks the soul, subdued by toil, to slumber,
  Its closing eye looks up to Thee in prayer;
Sweet the repose beneath the wings o'ershading,
  But sweeter still to wake and find Thee there.

So shall it be at last, in that bright morning
  When the soul waketh and life's shadows flee;
O, in that hour, fairer than daylight dawning,
  Shall rise the glorious thought, *I am with Thee!*

Harriet Beecher Stowe

XII
WITH THANKFUL HEARTS

434 *God, You Have Been Too Good to Me*

God, You have been too good to me,
You don't know what You've done.
A clod's too small to drink in all
The treasure of the sun.

The pitcher fills the lifted cup
And still the blessings pour
They overbrim the shallow rim
With cool refreshing store.

You are too prodigal with joy,
Too careless of its worth,
To let the stream with crystal gleam
Fall wasted on the earth.

Let many thirsty lips draw near
And quaff the greater part!
There still will be too much for me
To hold in one glad heart.

Charles Wharton Stork

435 *In Thankfull Remembrance for My Dear Husband's Safe Arrivall Sept. 3, 1662*

What shall I render to thy Name,
Or how thy Praises speak;
My thankes how shall I testefye?
O Lord, thou know'st I'm weak.

❈

What did I ask for but thou gav'st?
What could I more desire?
But Thankfullnes, even all my dayes,
I humbly this Require.

Thy mercyes, Lord, have been so great,
In number numberles,
Impossible for to recount
Or any way expresse.

Anne Bradstreet

436 *Thanksgiving*

Thank Thee, O Giver of life, O God!
For the force that flames in the winter sod;
For the breath in my nostrils, fiercely good,
The sweet of water, the taste of food;
The sun that silvers the pantry floor,
The step of a neighbor at my door;
For dusk that fondles the window-pane,
For the beautiful sound of falling rain.

Thank Thee for love and light and air,
For children's faces, keenly fair;
For the wonderful joy of perfect rest
When the sun's wick lowers within the West;
For huddling hills in gowns of snow
Warming themselves in the afterglow;
For Thy mighty wings that are never furled,
Bearing onward the rushing world.

Thank Thee, O Giver of Life, O God!
For Thy glory leaping the lightning-rod;
For Thy terrible spaces of love and fire
Where sparks from the forge of Thy desire
Storm through the void in floods of suns,
Far as the heat of Thy Presence runs,
And where hurricanes of chanting spheres
Swing to the pulse of the flying years.

Thank Thee for human toil that thrills
With the plan of Thine which man fulfills;

For bridges and tunnels, for ships that soar,
For iron and steel and the furnace roar;
For this anguished vortex of blood and pain
Where sweat and struggle are never vain;
For progress, pushing the teeming earth
On and up to a higher birth.
Thank Thee for life, for life, for *life*,
O Giver of life, O God!

Angela Morgan

437

From *A Thanksgiving*

For the rosebud's break of beauty
  Along the toiler's way;
For the violet's eye that opens
  To bless the new-born day;
For the bare twigs that in summer
  Bloom like the prophet's rod;
For the blossoming of flowers,
  I thank Thee, O my God!

For the lifting up of mountains,
  In brightness and in dread;
For the peaks where snow and sunshine
  Alone have dared to tread;
For the dark of silent gorges,
  Whence mighty cedars nod;
For the majesty of mountains,
  I thank Thee, O my God!

For the splendor of the sunsets,
  Vast mirrored on the sea;
For the gold-fringed clouds, that curtain
  Heaven's inner mystery;
For the molten bars of twilight,
  Where thought leans, glad, yet awed;
For the glory of the sunsets,
  I thank Thee, O my God!

For the earth, and all its beauty;
  The sky, and all its light;
For the dim and soothing shadows
  That rest the dazzled sight;
For unfading fields and prairies
  Where sense in vain has trod;
For the world's exhaustless beauty,
  I thank Thee, O my God!

Lucy Larcom

438 *Thankfulness*

My God, I thank Thee who hast made
  The Earth so bright;
So full of splendour and of joy,
  Beauty and light;
So many glorious things are here,
  Noble and right!

I thank Thee, too, that Thou hast made
  Joy to abound;
So many gentle thoughts and deeds
  Circling us round,
That in the darkest spot of Earth
  Some love is found.

I thank Thee *more* that all our joy
  Is touched with pain;
That shadows fall on brightest hours;
  That thorns remain;
So that Earth's bliss may be our guide,
  And not our chain.

For Thou who knowest, Lord, how soon
  Our weak heart clings,

Hast given us joys, tender and true,
Yet all with wings,
So that we see, gleaming on high,
Diviner things!

I thank Thee, Lord, that Thou hast kept
The best in store;
We have enough, yet not too much
To long for more:
A yearning for a deeper peace,
Not known before.

I thank Thee, Lord, that here our souls,
Though amply blest,
Can never find, although they seek,
A perfect rest—
Nor ever shall, until they lean
On Jesus' breast!

Adelaide Anne Procter

439 *To the Spirit Great and Good*

To the Spirit great and good,
Felt, although not understood,—
By whose breath, and in whose eyes,
The green earth rolls in the blue skies,—
Who we know, from things that bless,
Must delight in loveliness;
And who, therefore, we believe,
Means us well in things that grieve,—
Gratitude! Gratitude!
Heav'n be praised as heavenly should
Not with slavery, or with fears,
But with a face as towards a friend, and with thin sparkling tears.

Leigh Hunt

440 *Thanksgiving Day*

For all the gracious gifts in harvests fair
In things material whose goodly share
        I richly prize;
For man's abundant wealth that lies in sight,
And for the sense of power and of might
With which to meet my foe, and fight the fight,
        My thanks arise.

But for the richer gifts of Love and Peace
That bring the soul a sense of sweet release
        From pressing care;
For mercies shown; for greater growth of soul;
For light when clouds of deadly dark uproll
To point the way to some more loftly goal,
        And lead us there;

For broader human sympathy; for tears
Of Brotherhood to ease another's fears,
        And cheer his way;
For seeing eyes; and shoulders fit to bear
The burdens of our fellows in despair,
And right good will to help them in their care
        When times are gray;

For men of heart and soul inclined
To honors of a lowlier, meeker kind,
        With grace endued;
Who seek all dire injustices to mend,
To guide the hopeless to some hopeful end,
Not this alone, but all my days, I spend
        In gratitude!

John Kendrick Bangs

441 *Not Alone for Mighty Empire*

Not alone for mighty empire,
  Stretching far o'er land and sea,
Not alone for bounteous harvests,
  Lift we up our hearts to Thee.
Standing in the living present,
  Memory and hope between,
Lord, we would with deep thanksgiving
  Praise Thee more for things unseen.

Not for battle-ships and fortress,
  Not for conquests of the sword,
But for conquests of the spirit
  Give we thanks to Thee, O Lord;
For the heritage of freedom,
  For the home, the church, the school,
For the open door to manhood
  In a land the people rule.

For the armies of the faithful,
  Lives that passed and left no name;
For the glory that illumines
  Patriot souls of deathless fame;
For the people's prophet-leaders,
  Loyal to Thy living word,—
For all heroes of the spirit,
  Give we thanks to Thee, O Lord.

God of justice, save the people
  From the war of race and creed,
From the strife of class and faction,—
  Make our nation free indeed;
Keep her faith in simple manhood
  Strong as when her life began,
Till it find its full fruition
  In the Brotherhood of Man!

William Pierson Merrill

442 *Hymn* from *Bitter-Sweet*

For Summer's bloom and Autumn's blight,
  For bending wheat and blasted maize,
For health and sickness, Lord of light,
  And Lord of darkness, hear our praise!

We trace to Thee our joys and woes,—
  To Thee of causes still the cause,—
We thank Thee that Thy hand bestows;
  We bless Thee that Thy love withdraws.

We bring no sorrows to Thy throne;
  We come to Thee with no complaint;
In Providence Thy will is done,
  And that is sacred to the saint.

Here on this blest Thanksgiving Night;
  We raise to Thee our grateful voice;
For what Thou doest, Lord, is right;
  And thus believing, we rejoice.

Josiah Gilbert Holland

443 *Thanksgiving*

Lord, I give thanks!
Last year Thou knowest my best ambitions failed,
My back with scourgings of defeat was flailed,
My eyes felt oft the sharp, salt wash of tears,
No guerdon blessed the tireless toil of years,
Fast in the snares my helpless feet were tied,
Yet in my woes Thou didst with me abide—
Lord, I give thanks!

Lord, I give thanks!
Last year my one lone ship came back to me,
A ruined wreck of what she used to be,

No cargo in her hold, storm-stained and scarred,
Oh, Lord, Thou knowest that it was hard, was hard,
To watch her drifting hulk with hopeless eye,
Yet, in my desolation Thou wert nigh—
Lord, I give thanks!

Lord, I give thanks!
Last year the one I loved the dearest died,
And like a desert waste became the wide,
And weary world. Love's last sweet star went out,
Blackness of darkness wrapped me round about,
Yet in the midst of my mad misery,
Thou lentest Thy rod and staff to comfort me—
Lord, I give thanks!

Susie M. Best

444 *I Have a Roof*

Lord, I am poor; but it becomes
The poorest heart to count its store.
And therefore I upon this tide
Will turn and tell my blessings o'er.

I have a roof, made snug and tight,
That shelters me; a window where
I see the seasons framed in turn
And find each in its fashion fair;
A door thro' which no harm has stepped,
Walls where my well-loved pictures bide;
A-many books, a pot of flowers,
A deep chair by a warm fireside.

I have brave hopes, a quiet mind
And many a gentle memory;
An old dog in whose faithful eyes
I have attained divinity;

The joy of waking wings is mine,
The grace of sleep at daylight's end,
The trust of little children and
The honest handclasp of a friend;

A tree, a garden and my food;
Much laughter, peaceful silences;
A heart that is not yet too old
To take delight where Beauty is;
Strong hands, sound wits and health enough;
Pride in a comely task well done,
And—binding all my blessings in
To one fair sheaf—the love of one
Who, with no thought of self, would break
His dearest dream to serve my need—

Lord, with my reckoning half told
I know that I am rich indeed.

Ada Jackson

445

Thanksgiving

Now gracious plenty rules the board,
 And in the purse is gold;
By multitudes in glad accord
 Thy giving is extolled.
Ah, suffer *me* to thank thee, Lord,
 For what Thou dost withhold!

I thank Thee that howe'er we climb
 There yet is something higher;
That though through all our reach of time
 We to the stars aspire,
Still, still beyond us burns sublime
 The pure sidereal fire!

I thank Thee for the unexplained,
The hope that lies before,
The victory that is not gained,—
O Father, more and more
I thank Thee for the unattained,
The good we hunger for!

I thank Thee for the voice that sings
To inner depths of being;
For all the upward spread of wings,
From earthly bondage freeing;
For mystery—the dream of things
Beyond our power of seeing!

Florence Earle Coates

446 *The Things I Miss*

An easy thing, O Power Divine,
To thank Thee for these gifts of Thine!
For summer's sunshine, winter's snow,
For hearts that kindle, thoughts that glow.
But when shall I attain to this,—
To thank Thee for the things I miss?

For all young Fancy's early gleams,
The dreamed-of joys that still are dreams,
Hopes unfulfilled, and pleasures known
Through others' fortunes, not my own,
And blessings seen that are not given,
And never will be, this side of heaven.

Had I too, shared the joys I see,
Would there have been a heaven for me?
Could I have felt Thy presence near?
Had I possessed what I held dear?
My deepest fortune, highest bliss,
Have grown perchance from things I miss.

Sometimes there comes an hour of calm;
Grief turns to blessing, pain to balm;
A Power that works above my will
Still leads me onward, upward still.
And then my heart attains to this,—
To thank Thee for the things I miss.

Thomas Wentworth Higginson

447 *A Thanksgiving*

Lord, in this dust Thy sovereign voice
First quicken'd love divine;
I am all Thine,—Thy care and choice,
My very praise is Thine.

I praise Thee, while Thy providence
In childhood frail I trace,
For blessings given, ere dawning sense
Could seek or scan Thy grace;

Blessings in boyhood's marvelling hour,
Bright dreams, and fancyings strange;
Blessings, when reason's awful power
Gave thought a bolder range;

Blessings of friends, which to my door
Unask'd, unhoped, have come;
And, choicer still, a countless store
Of eager smiles at home.

Yet, Lord, in memory's fondest place
I shrine those seasons sad,
When, looking up, I saw Thy face
In kind austereness clad.

I would not miss one sigh or tear,
Heart-pang, or throbbing brow;

Sweet was the chastisement severe,
And sweet its memory now.

Yes! let the fragrant scars abide,
Love-tokens in Thy stead,
Faint shadows of the spear-pierced side
And thorn-encompass'd head.

And such Thy tender force be still,
When self would swerve or stray,
Shaping to truth the froward will
Along Thy narrow way.

Deny me wealth; far, far remove
The lure of power or name;
Hope thrives in straits, in weakness love,
And faith in this world's shame.

John Henry Newman

448

Grace

How much, preventing God, how much I owe
To the defences thou hast round me set;
Example, custom, fear, occasion slow,—
These scorned bondmen were my parapet.
I dare not peep over this parapet
To gauge with glance the roaring gulf below,
The depths of sin to which I had descended,
Had not these me against myself defended.

Ralph Waldo Emerson

449

Thanksgiving

I

Lord, for the erring thought
Not into evil wrought:
Lord, for the wicked will

Betrayed and baffled still:
For the heart from itself kept,
Our thanksgiving accept.

II

For ignorant hopes that were
Broken to our blind prayer:
For pain, death, sorrow, sent
Unto our chastisement:
For all loss of seeming good,
Quicken our gratitude.

William Dean Howells

450 *A Grace*

Reveal Thy Presence now, O Lord,
As in the Upper Room of old;
Break Thou our bread, grace Thou our board,
And keep our hearts from growing cold.

Thomas Tiplady

451 *A Poet's Grace*

Before Meat

O Thou, who kindly doth provide
For ev'ry creature's want!
We bless the God of Nature wide
For all Thy goodness lent.
And if it please Thee, heavenly Guide,
May never worse be sent;
But, whether granted or denied,
Lord, bless us with content.

After Meat

O Thou, in whom we live and move,
Who made the sea and shore,
Thy goodness constantly we prove,

And, grateful, would adore;
And, if it please Thee, Power above!
Still grant us with such store
The friend we trust, the fair we love,
And we desire no more.

Robert Burns

452

Prayer before Meat

Christ, by dark clouds of worldliness concealed,
Stand in the breaking of this bread revealed;
Feeling Thy tender presence let us guard
Each cruel thought, each bitter, unkind word.
Linked here by bonds of love, now let us feed
Upon Thy grace and find it meat indeed.

Una W. Harsen

453

Grace at Evening

For all the beauties of the day,
The innocence of childhood's play,
For health and strength and laughter sweet,
Dear Lord, our thanks we now repeat.

For this our daily gift of food
We offer now our gratitude,
For all the blessings we have known
Our debt of gratefulness we own.

Here at the table now we pray,
Keep us together down the way;
May this, our family circle, be
Held fast by love and unity.

Grant, when the shades of night shall fall,
Sweet be the dreams of one and all;

And when another day shall break
Unto Thy service may we wake.

Edgar A. Guest

454 *Grace at Evening*

Be with us, Lord, at eventide;
  Far has declined the day,
Our hearts have glowed
Along the road,
  Thou hast made glad our way.

Take Thou this loaf and bless it, Lord,
  And then with us partake;
Unveil our eyes
To recognize
  Thyself, for Thy dear sake.

Edwin McNeill Poteat

EPILOGUE

PRAYER-POEMS ON PRAYER

455 *Sonnet*

Lord, what a change within us one short hour
Spent in thy presence will prevail to make,
What heavy burdens from our bosoms take,
What parchéd grounds refresh, as with a shower!
We kneel, and all around us seems to lower;
We rise, and all, the distant and the near,
Stands forth in sunny outline, brave and clear;
We kneel how weak, we rise how full of power.
Why therefore should we do ourselves this wrong
Or others—that we are not always strong,
That we are ever overborne with care,
That we should ever weak or heartless be,
Anxious or troubled, when with us is prayer,
And joy and strength and courage are with Thee?

Richard Chenevix Trench

456 *The Taste of Prayer*

Lord, lay the taste of prayer upon my tongue,
And let my lips speak banquets unto Thee;
Then may this richest feast, when once begun,
Keep me in hunger through eternity.

Ralph W. Seager

457 *To the Supreme Being*

The prayers I make will then be sweet indeed
If Thou the spirit give by which I pray:
My unassisted heart is barren clay,
That of its native self can nothing feed:

Of good and pious works thou art the seed,
That quickens only where thou say'st it may:
Unless Thou show to us thine own true way
No man can find it: Father! Thou must lead.
Do Thou, then, breathe those thoughts into my mind
By which such virtue may in me be bred
That in thy holy footsteps I may tread;
The fetters of my tongue do Thou unbind,
That I may have the power to sing of thee,
And sound thy praises everlastingly.

Michelangelo Buonarroti
Tr. William Wordsworth

458 *The Cell*

When from the hush of this cool wood
  I go, Lord, to the noisy mart,
Give me among the multitude,
  I pray, a lonely heart.

Yes, build in me a secret cell
  Where quietness shall be a song:
In that green solitude I'll dwell,
  And praise Thee all day long.

George Rostrevor

459 *Prayer*

I ask good things that I detest,
  With speeches fair;
Heed not, I pray Thee, Lord, my breast,
  But hear my prayer.

I say ill things I would not say—
  Things unaware:
Regard my breast, Lord, in Thy day,
  And not my prayer.

My heart is evil in Thy sight:
My good thoughts flee:
O Lord, I cannot wish aright—
Wish Thou for me.

O bend my words and acts to Thee,
However ill,
That I, whate'er I say or be,
May serve Thee still.

O let my thoughts abide in Thee
Lest I should fall:
Show me Thyself in all I see,
Thou Lord of all.

Robert Louis Stevenson

460 *I Dare Not Pray to Thee*

I dare not pray to thee, for thou art won
Rarely by those by whom thou hast been wooed;
Thou comest unsolicited, unsued,
Like sudden splendours of the midnight sun.

Yet in my heart the hope doth still abide
That thou hast haply heard my unbreathed prayer;
That in the stifling moment of despair,
I shall turn round and find thee by my side.

Like a sad pilgrim who has wandered far,
And hopes not any longer for the day,
But blinded by black thickets finds no way,

Comes to a rift of trees in that sad plight,
And suddenly sees the unending aisles of night
And in the emerald gloom the morning star.

Maurice Baring

INDEXES

INDEX OF TITLES

(References are to poem numbers. First-line titles are listed in the Index of First Lines.)

INDEX OF FIRST LINES

(References are to poem numbers.)

INDEX OF POETS

(References are to poem numbers.)

INDEX OF SPECIAL DAYS AND OCCASIONS

(References are to poem numbers.)

INDEX OF SUBJECTS

(References are to poem numbers.)